The Making
of a Manager

The Making of a Manager

What to Do When
Everyone Looks to You

Julie Zhuo

PORTFOLIO / PENGUIN

Portfolio/Penguin
An imprint of Penguin Random House LLC
penguinrandomhouse.com

Most Portfolio books are available at a discount when purchased in quantity
for sales promotions or corporate use. Special editions, which include
personalized covers, excerpts, and corporate imprints, can be created
when purchased in large quantities. For more information, please call
(212) 572-2232 or email specialmarkets@penguinrandomhouse.com.
Your local bookstore can also assist with discounted bulk purchases using
the Penguin Random House corporate Business-to-Business program.
For assistance in locating a participating retailer, email
B2B@penguinrandomhouse.com.

LIBRARY OF CONGRESS CATALOGING-IN-PUBLICATION DATA
Names: Zhuo, Julie, author.
Title: The making of a manager : what to do when everyone looks to you /
Julie Zhuo.
Description: New York : Portfolio/Penguin, [2019] | Includes bibliographical
references and index.
Identifiers: LCCN 2018041569 (print) | LCCN 2018042422 (ebook) |
ISBN 9780735219571 (Ebook) | ISBN 9780735219564 (hardcover) |
ISBN 9780525540427 (international edition)
Subjects: LCSH: Zhuo, Julie. | Executive ability. | Teams in the workplace—
Management. | Management. | Leadership. | Women executives—
United States.
Classification: LCC HD38.2 (ebook) | LCC HD38.2 .Z48 2019 (print) |
DDC 658.4/09--dc23
LC record available at https://lccn.loc.gov/2018041569

Printed in the United States of America
10 9 8 7 6 5 4 3 2 1

Book design by Sabrina Bowers

To Mike, with whom I manage this beautiful life

Contents

The Making
of a Manager

Great Managers Are Made, Not Born

THE MYTH

THE REALITY

I remember the meeting when my manager asked me to become a manager.

It was unexpected, like going for your daily run and tripping over a pirate chest. *Oh*, I thought, *how intriguing*.

We were sitting in a ten-person conference room, kitty-corner from each other. "Our team is growing," my manager explained. "We need another manager, and you get along with everyone. What do you think?"

I was twenty-five, working at a start-up. All that I knew of management could be neatly summarized into two words: *meetings* and *PROMOTION*. I mean, this was a promotion, wasn't it? Everyone knows this conversation is the equivalent of Harry Potter getting a visit from Hagrid on a dark and stormy night, the first step in an adventurous and fulfilling career. I wasn't about to turn down that kind of invitation.

So I said yes.

It was only later, walking out of the room, that I thought about the details of what she had said. *I got along with everyone.* Surely there was more to management than that. How much more? I was about to find out.

———

I remember my first meeting with a direct report.

I arrived five minutes past our scheduled time, in a rush and flustered by my lateness. *This is a terrible start*, I thought to myself.

I could see him through the windowed door of the conference room—the same one I had met my manager in previously—eyes glued to his phone. Just a day earlier, we had both been designers on the same team, sitting in our adjacent pods, working on our respective projects while lobbing rapid-fire design feedback across the aisle. Then the announcement was made, and now I was his manager.

I'm not nervous, I told myself. *We're going to have a great conversation.* About what, I wasn't entirely sure. I just wanted this meeting to feel normal, like it had yesterday and the day before that. If he didn't *love* the fact that I was his manager, then at the very least I wanted him to be cool with it.

I'm not nervous.

I walked in. He glanced up from his phone, and I'll never forget the expression on his face. It had all the surliness of a teenager forced to attend his ten-year-old cousin's Pokémon-themed birthday party.

"Hi," I said, trying to keep my voice level. "So, uh, what are you working on right now?"

His scowl only deepened, settling in like a bear for the winter. I could feel the sweat starting to form on my face, the hot rush of blood pounding in my ears.

I wasn't a better designer than this guy. I wasn't smarter or more experienced. The look on his face alone was enough to dispel me of any notion that he'd "be cool" with the fact that I was his manager. The message was as clear as if it had been written in giant black Sharpie:

You have no idea what you're doing.

At that moment, I felt he was absolutely right.

—

By all accounts, the path that led me to managing Facebook's design team was an unlikely one. I grew up in the dense streets of

Shanghai and then the humid suburbs of Houston, an immigrant clueless about the significance of *Star Wars*, Michael Jackson, and *E.T.* Growing up, I'd heard the term *Silicon Valley* a few times but took it literally. I imagined that nestled between two mountain ranges were neat little rows of factories printing silicon chips like Hershey bars. If you had asked me what designers do, I would have said, "Make nice clothing."

I did know two things, though, even early on, and those were how much I loved drawing and building. There is a photo of me at eight years old on Christmas morning, a huge grin stretched across my face as I held up the present I'd been begging for all year: a new set of pirate LEGOS—complete with a monkey and a shark!

In middle school, my best friend Marie and I passed each other notebooks filled with elaborate doodles between classes. In high school, we discovered the magic of HTML, which let us combine our hobbies of drawing and building into the perfect pastime: making websites showcasing our illustrations. I could think of no better way to spend spring break than obsessively following the latest online Photoshop tutorials ("How to Achieve Realistic Skin Tones") or redesigning my website to show off a new JavaScript trick (links that glowed when you moused over them).

When I arrived at Stanford, I knew I wanted to study computer science. So I took classes on algorithms and databases in preparation for a job at seasoned, polished Microsoft or quirky, up-and-coming Google, where many former classmates had gone. But by sophomore year, a new craze was sweeping through Stanford. "Imagine!" we chattered excitedly in hallways and over meals. "A site where you check out photos of that crush from organic chemistry, or get to know your dorm mates' favorite bands, or leave cryptic messages on your friends' 'Walls'!"

I was hooked. Facebook was unlike anything I had used before. It felt like a living thing, a dynamic version of our college selves that extended into the online world and helped us get to know each other in new ways.

I'd heard Facebook was founded by some Harvard dropouts, but I didn't know much about start-ups until I took a class my senior year about Silicon Valley entrepreneurship. And then I understood: Oh, this was the land of hungry, foolish dreamers who were given the chance to build their version of the future with a little help from venture capitalist fairy godparents. This was the land of innovations borne from a mix of smart minds, iron resolve, lucky timing, and a whole lot of duct tape.

If I was going to do this start-up thing at any point in my life, why not now, when I was young with nothing to lose? And why not with a product that I used every day and loved? A good friend of mine, Wayne Chang, had joined Facebook six months earlier, and he couldn't stop talking it up. "Just come check it out," he cajoled. "At least do an internship and see what the company is like."

I took his advice and interviewed. Soon, I found myself in the graffitied lobby on my first day as Facebook's first-ever engineering intern. The entire company at the time could fit into a backyard party. News Feed was not yet a concept, and nobody knew our service except high school and college students. In the world of social networking, we were dwarfed by the juggernaut MySpace, with its 150 million users.

And yet, as small as we were, our dreams were enormous. We cranked out code into the late hours of the night while Daft Punk blared from the speakers. *One day*, we told ourselves, *we'll be bigger than MySpace*—and then, laughing a little because it sounded so ludicrous—*we'll eventually connect the world*.

Two months into my internship, I decided to stay full time. And because I knew Photoshop from my drawing days, my friend Ruchi Sanghvi suggested that I sit with the designers and get involved in deciding what to put on the screen. *Huh. Designing websites is a real profession?* I thought. *Count me in!*

Because we were a start-up, nobody thought it was weird that I was suddenly showing my own design proposals for new features. We were all wearing many hats then, tackling problems as we saw them, diving in and out of code and pixels and back to code again. And so, rather by accident than by any masterful plan, I added a new hat to my rotation: *designer*.

Three years later, after that fateful conversation with my manager, my role shifted again. Our design team had almost doubled in size since I'd started. Having made it through my first few years at a hyper-growth start-up, I thought I was used to change. I was no stranger to dealing with the firsts or rolling with the punches.

Still, I was unprepared for just how much the new manager role would stretch me. For one thing, I was managing product designers, a discipline I didn't even know existed before I arrived at the company. For another, the responsibilities of managing people and the way they worked together felt like an enormous leap from creating user interfaces or writing code. In those early months and years, everything felt new and uncomfortable.

I remember my first time interviewing someone for my team. Even though I was clearly the one with the upper hand—*I* asked the questions, *I* decided how the conversation should flow, *I* selected *hire* or *no hire* at the end of the day—my hands were shaking for the entire forty-five minutes. What if the candidate thought my questions were stupid? What if she saw me for the fraud I felt like? What if I accidentally made our team seem like a clown show?

I remember my first time delivering bad news. We were kicking off an exciting new project that had everyone passionately discussing the possibilities. Two of my reports asked me if they could be the lead. I had to say no to someone. I practiced the conversation in front of my bathroom mirror at home, imagining every terrible scenario—was this even the right decision? Was I a dream crusher? Would somebody quit on me right on the spot?

I remember my first time presenting in front of a large audience. I was showcasing design work at Facebook's F8 conference amid a sea of fuzzy cushions and neon lights. We'd never done a public event at that scale before, so it was a big deal. In the weeks leading up to the event, I couldn't stop fiddling with every detail of my presentation. I desperately wanted it to go well, but public speaking terrified me. Even practicing my talk in front of helpful colleagues felt like a nerve-racking ordeal.

I remember my three primary emotions navigating the choppy waters of my new role: fear, doubt, and *am I crazy for feeling this way?* Everyone else around me seemed to be doing just fine. Everyone else made it look easy.

I never thought managing was easy. I still don't.

Today, nearly ten years after I started on that path, my team has grown by a few orders of magnitude. We design the experience that more than two billion people see when they tap the blue *f* icon on their phones. We think through the details of how people share what's on their minds, keep up with their friends, interact through conversations and thumbs-ups, and create communities together. If we do our jobs well, then people all over the world—from Belgium to Kenya, from India to Argentina—will feel closer to one another.

Good design at its core is about understanding people and their needs in order to create the best possible tools for them. I'm drawn to design for a lot of the same reasons that I'm drawn to management—it feels like a deeply human endeavor to empower others.

I'm by no means a management expert. I've learned largely by doing, and despite my best intentions, I've made countless mistakes. But this is how anything in life goes: You try something. You figure out what worked and what didn't. You file away lessons for the future. And then you get better. Rinse, repeat.

I've had plenty of help, too, in the form of some amazing leadership training courses (Crucial Conversations is my favorite), articles and books that I turn to again and again (like *High Output Management* and *How to Win Friends and Influence People*), and, most important of all, my colleagues. They have generously shared their wisdom with me and inspired me to strive for better. I feel lucky to have worked with Mark Zuckerberg, Sheryl Sandberg, and a host of others past and present who have taught me so much.

Another tactic in my self-education started about four years ago, when I decided to write a blog. I thought that the act of sitting down every week and sorting through the jumble of thoughts ping-ponging around my head would help me make sense of them.

I called my blog *The Year of the Looking Glass* because, like Alice, "I know who I *was* when I got up this morning, but I think I must have been changed several times since then." One day, far in the future, I imagined looking back on my collection of posts and recalling my journey. *Here were all the things I struggled with. Here are all the ways I have learned.*

Other people began to read my articles. They sent them to their friends and colleagues. Strangers started approaching me at events and conferences to discuss the things I had written. They told me how much they appreciated the way I had broken down the struggle. Many were new managers. Some were experienced but dealing with similar challenges of growth and scale. And others weren't currently managers but wondered if it was something they wanted to do down the road.

"You should write a book," some folks suggested. I'd laugh it off. They couldn't be serious! I had so much left to learn. Maybe someday, in the twilight of my career, after I had discovered the true secret to great management, I could cozy up in a plaid armchair next to a roaring fire and jot down all the heaps of wisdom I had accumulated.

I told my friend this, and he rolled his eyes. "Yeah, but at that point, you won't remember what it's like at the beginning, when everything feels new and hard and crazy. You'll be so far removed." He had a point. There are plenty of management books out there written by top CEOs and leadership experts. Countless resources exist for executives who want to become even more effective through learning about the latest organizational research or business trends.

But most managers are not CEOs or senior executives. Most lead smaller teams, and sometimes not even directly. Most are not featured in the pages of *Forbes* or *Fortune*. But they are managers all the same, and they share a common purpose: helping a group of people achieve a common goal. These managers may be teachers or principals, captains or coaches, administrators or planners.

When I considered this, I thought, *Maybe I can write this book, because it's more relevant for a certain group of people now*: new managers thrown into the deep end, overwhelmed managers wondering how to best help their reports, managers dealing with fast-growing teams, or those simply curious about management. I was one of them not so long ago.

Running a team is hard because it ultimately boils down to people, and all of us are multifaceted and complex beings. Just like how there is no one way to go about being a person, there is no one way to go about managing a group of people.

And yet, working together in teams is how the world moves forward. We can create things far grander and more ambitious than anything we could have done alone. This is how battles are won, how innovation moves forward, how organizations succeed. This is how any remarkable achievement happens.

I believe this as deeply as I believe anything: Great managers are made, not born. It doesn't matter who you are. If you care enough to be reading this, then you care enough to be a great manager.

Dear reader, I hope that this book gives you useful tips for your day-to-day. But more importantly, I hope this book helps you understand the *whys* of management, because only when you've bought into the *whys* can you truly be effective in the *hows*. Why do managers even exist? Why should you have one-on-one meetings with your reports? Why should you hire Candidate A over Candidate B? Why do so many managers make the same mistakes?

Some of the stories and perspectives I describe may be unique to the environment I work in, which is a tech start-up that became a Fortune 500 company. Maybe you will only need to hire someone new once in a blue moon. Maybe meetings won't be a big part of your day. Still, much of the daily work of managers—giving feedback, creating a healthy culture, planning for the future—is universal.

Finally, I hope that this book can be a resource on your shelf, the kind of thing you can read in any order, flip back to at any time, and reread when you suddenly see a part of your role in a new light.

Though I'm a designer, this is not a book about how to build products. You won't find deep reflections on what makes for great design or what I think of social media. I won't sit here and tell you the story of Facebook.

This is a book about how someone with no formal training learned to become a confident manager. This is the book I wish I had in my first few years, with all my fears and doubts and am-I-crazies.

This is the book that's here to tell you that your fears and doubts are normal, and, like me, you're going to figure it out.

Ready? Let's get started.

Chapter One

What Is Management?

AVOID

ASPIRE

In May of 2006, when I first started my job, I didn't know what I didn't know.

On the one hand, given that Facebook was a social network for college and high school students at the time, I thought that in some ways I was the perfect candidate. I mean, who knew Facebook's audience better than a recent grad like myself? I was hungry to make my mark on the world, and there was nothing to weigh me down. I had no institutionalized doctrines, no tragic failures to speak of. And after four years of cramming for exams, writing countless papers, and pulling all-nighter coding marathons, hard work and I got along just fine.

But I faced some major disadvantages as well, the biggest being that I had very little experience under my belt. Like in most start-ups, our team was focused primarily on getting things done, not on organizational hierarchy. I didn't have a formal manager until about a year in, when one of the senior designers on our team, Rebekah, took on that role. Before that, we were operating as a loose collective, everyone just helping out where they were needed. Two years later, suddenly *I* was a manager.

I had a lot to learn. But when I look back now, what surprises me the most is how little I understood of what *management* was all about.

Oh, we're all familiar with good and bad managers, from James Bond's M to *A Christmas Carol*'s Ebenezer Scrooge, from Katharine Graham in *The Post* to Miranda Priestly in *The Devil Wears Prada*.

It's not as if managers are some sort of rare, exotic species. Most people have one. At the dinner table growing up, I remember my parents—an IT specialist and a stockbroker—talking about what their bosses did or said that day. I had managers who'd shown me the ropes during my high school and college teaching jobs.

But if you had asked me what I thought a manager's job was before I started, here's what I would have said.

A MANAGER'S JOB IS TO . . .

* have meetings with reports to help them solve their problems,
* share feedback about what is or isn't going well, and
* figure out who should be promoted and who should be fired.

Fast-forward three years. Having done the job now, I'm a bit wiser. My revised answer would look like the following.

A MANAGER'S JOB IS TO . . .

* build a team that works well together,
* support members in reaching their career goals, and
* create processes to get work done smoothly and efficiently.

As you can see, my answers evolved from basic, day-to-day activities (having meetings and giving feedback) to longer-term goals (building teams and supporting career growth). The new answers sound smarter and more grown-up. Go, me!

Except . . . they're still not quite right. You might be thinking, *Well, what's wrong with these answers?* Great managers certainly do all the things on both lists.

True, but the problem is that these answers are still an assortment of activities. If I asked you, "What is the job of a soccer player?" would you say that it's to attend practices, pass the ball to their teammates, and attempt to score goals?

No, of course not. You'd tell me why those activities matter in the first place. You'd say, "The job of a soccer player is to win games."

So what is the job of a manager? Without understanding this deeply, it's hard to know how to be good at it.

That's what this first chapter is about.

THE ONE-LINE DEFINITION OF A MANAGER'S JOB

Imagine that you decide to set up a lemonade stand because you love lemonade and think it could be a great business.

In the beginning, what you need to do seems pretty clear. You go to the store and get yourself a knapsack full of lemons. You juice those lemons, dump in a generous helping of sugar, and add water. You get a folding table and a lounge chair, a pitcher, a cooler, and some cups. You decorate a lovely chalk sign announcing your delicious offering (and competitive pricing!), and then, near a busy intersection, you set up shop and cheerfully ask if any passersby are thirsty.

It's simple when it's just you. It's your hands that squeezed the lemons, your feet that trudged from the store to the kitchen to your stand, your arms that lugged the pitcher and cooler. If the chalkboard handwriting looks sloppy, that's on you. If your lemonade is too sweet or sour, you have only yourself to blame. Nothing will get done unless you choose to do it.

But great news! Beyoncé drops an album and suddenly everyone is obsessed with lemonade! As soon as you sell a glass, ten other people are crowded around your stand, eager for a gulp of that refreshing, nostalgic beverage. You can't keep up with demand, so you decide to enlist the help of your neighbors Henry and Eliza. You'll pay them each a fair wage, and in exchange, they'll come work for you.

Congrats! You are now a manager!

"Duh," you say. "I hired them and I'm paying them money. I'm the CEO, the head honcho, the boss. Of course I'm a manager."

Actually, you'd be a manager even if you didn't hire them or pay them. The management aspect has nothing to do with employment status and everything to do with the fact that *you are no longer trying to get something done by yourself.*

With three pairs of hands and feet, you can make and sell lemonade so much faster. One of you can mix the drink while another collects payment. You can rotate shifts and keep the stand open for more hours. You might even have time to shop around for cheaper ingredients.

At the same time, you're giving up some level of control. You won't get to make every decision anymore. When things go badly, it might not be because of anything *you* did. If Eliza forgets to add the sugar, you'll get a lot of puckered, unhappy customers. If Henry's scowl intimidates others, you'll get fewer people stopping for a drink.

You felt the trade-offs were worth it. Why? Because your goal is the same as when you started: You love lemonade and think it could be a great business. You believe more people should experience the wonders of your favorite drink, and with Eliza and Henry on board, you feel you're more likely to succeed.

This is the crux of management: It is the belief that a team of people can achieve more than a single person going it alone. It is the realization that you don't have to do everything yourself, be the best at everything yourself, or even know *how* to do everything yourself.

Your job, as a manager, is to *get better outcomes from a group of people working together.*

It's from this simple definition that everything else flows.

HOW DO YOU TELL A GREAT MANAGER FROM AN AVERAGE MANAGER?

I used to think judging whether a manager was great was like judging whether a fifteen-year-old was qualified to drive. There would be a series of tests, and each successful demonstration would earn a satisfying *check.* Are they well regarded by other people? Can they solve big, strategic problems? Do they give killer presentations? Can they knock out twenty important tasks in a day? Reply to emails while waiting in line for coffee? Defuse a tense situation? Always be closing? Etc., etc.

These are all wonderful qualities to have in a manager, to be sure, and we'll discuss many of them later on, but the litmus test of whether or not a manager is excelling doesn't need to be so complex.

If the job is defined as getting better outcomes from a group of people working together, then a great manager's team will consistently achieve great outcomes.

If the outcome you care about is building a thriving lemonade business, then a great manager's team will turn a higher profit than a mediocre manager's team. A bad manager's team loses money.

If the outcome you care about is educating children, then a great manager's team will better prepare students for the future than an average manager's team. A bad manager's team fails to give kids the skills and knowledge they need to thrive.

If the outcome you care about is getting amazing design, then a great manager's team will consistently deliver concepts that wow. A mediocre manager's team will produce work that gets the job done but doesn't stand out. A bad manager's team will regularly suggest proposals that make you think, *Surely we can do better than this.*

Andy Grove, founder and CEO of Intel and a legendary manager of his time, wrote that when it comes to evaluations, one should look at "the *output* of the work unit and not simply the *activity* involved. Obviously, you measure a salesman by the orders he gets (output), not by the calls he makes (activity)."

You can be the smartest, most well-liked, most hardworking manager in the world, but if your team has a long-standing reputation for mediocre outcomes, then unfortunately you can't objectively be considered a "great" manager.

That said, at any given point in time, it can be hard to accurately judge. A great manager might be asked to lead a new team, and because it takes her time to ramp up, her results might be unimpressive at the beginning. On the flip side, a bad manager might achieve a few quarters of amazing results because she inherited a talented team or set high-pressure ultimatums that had people burning the midnight oil.

Time, however, always reveals the truth. The best employees don't tend to stick around for years and years under a boss who treats them poorly or whom they don't respect. And talented managers can typically turn around poor-performing teams if they are empowered to make changes.

Six years ago, I switched my reporting to a different manager, Chris Cox, Facebook's chief product officer. One of the earliest conversations I remember us having is when I asked him how he evaluates the job of a manager. He smiled and said, "My framework is quite simple." Half of what he looked at was my team's results—did we achieve our aspirations in creating valuable, easy-to-use, and well-crafted design work? The other half was based on the strength and satisfaction of my team—did I do a good job hiring and developing individuals, and was my team happy and working well together?

The first criterion looks at our team's present outcomes; the second criterion asks whether we're set up for great outcomes in the future.

I've gone on to adopt this framework for assessing managers on my own team. Being awesome at the job means playing the long game and building a reputation for excellence. Through thick or thin, in spite of the hundreds of things calling for your attention every day, never forget what you're ultimately here to do: help your team achieve great outcomes.

THE THREE THINGS MANAGERS THINK ABOUT ALL DAY

So how does a manager help a group of people achieve great outcomes?

When I was first starting out, my mind would have gone straight to the everyday duties—preparing for that next meeting, removing a roadblock for a report, coming up with an execution plan for the next month.

J. Richard Hackman, the leading scholar of teams, spent forty years trying to answer this question. He studied the ways professionals work together in hospitals, in symphony orchestras, and inside the cockpits of commercial airliners. One of his conclusions is that making a team function well is harder than it looks. "Research consistently shows that teams underperform, despite all the extra resources they have," he says. "That's because problems with coordination and motivation typically chip away at the benefits of collaboration."

Hackman's research describes five conditions that increase a team's odds of success: having a real team (one with clear boundaries and stable membership), a compelling direction, an enabling structure, a supportive organizational context, and expert coaching.

My own observations are similar, and I've come to think of the multitude of tasks that fill up a manager's day as sorting neatly into three buckets: *purpose*, *people*, and *process*.

The *purpose* is the outcome your team is trying to accomplish, otherwise known as the *why*. Why do you wake up and choose to do *this* thing instead of the thousands of other things you could be doing? Why pour your time and energy into this particular goal with this particular group of people? What would be different about the world if your team were wildly successful? Everyone on the team should have a similar picture of *why does our work matter*? If this purpose is missing or unclear, then you may experience conflicts or mismatched expectations.

For example, let's say your vision is to get a lemonade stand on every block, starting first in your city and then expanding throughout the country. However, your employee Henry is under the impression that your stand ought to be a popular hangout spot for the neighbors. He'll start doing things that you think are unimportant or wasteful, like buying a bunch of lawn chairs or trying to serve pizza along with lemonade. To prevent these misalignments, you'll need to get him and the other members of your team on board with what you truly care about.

At the same time, you can't simply *demand* that everyone believe in your vision. If Henry thinks your grand plan of "a lemonade stand on every block" is stupid, he won't be motivated to help you see it through. He might decide instead to join a venture he cares more about, like that pizza-and-pool parlor down the street.

The first big part of your job as a manager is to ensure that *your team knows what success looks like and cares about achieving it*. Getting everyone to understand and believe in your team's purpose, whether it's as specific as "make every customer who calls feel cared for" or as broad as "bring the world closer together," requires understanding and believing in it yourself, and then sharing it at every opportunity—from writing emails to setting goals, from checking in with a single report to hosting large-scale meetings.

The next important bucket that managers think about is *people*, otherwise known as the *who*. Are the members of your team set up to succeed? Do they have the right skills? Are they motivated to do great work?

If you don't have the right people for the job, or you don't have an environment where they can thrive, then you're going to have problems. For example, say Eliza doesn't precisely measure the right amount of lemon juice, sugar, and water for your secret formula, or Henry can't be bothered to greet customers politely, or you're terrible at planning. Your lemonade stand will suffer. To manage people well, you must develop trusting relationships with them, understand their strengths and weaknesses (as well as your own), make good decisions about who should do what (including hiring and firing when necessary), and coach individuals to do their best.

Finally, the last bucket is *process*, which describes *how* your team works together. You might have a superbly talented team with a very clear understanding of what the end goal is, but if it's not apparent how everyone's supposed to work together or what the team's values are, then even simple tasks can get enormously complicated. Who should do what by when? What principles should govern decision-making?

For example, say it's Henry's job to pick up lemonade ingredients from the store and it's Eliza's job to make the lemonade. How will Henry know when he needs to make a run? How will Eliza find the supplies? What should happen if lemons run out on a particularly hot day? If there isn't a predictable plan, Henry and Eliza will waste time coordinating handoffs and dealing with the inevitable mistakes that arise.

Often, people have an allergic reaction to the word *process*. For me, it used to conjure up the feeling of glacial progress. I imagined myself flailing around in huge stacks of paperwork, my calendar filled with tedious meetings. In a processless world, I imagined myself free to do whatever was needed to make things happen *quickly*, with no red tape, no barriers, no overhead.

There's some truth to this. We've already established that when you are working by yourself, you get to make all the decisions. You are limited only by how fast you can think and act.

In a team setting, it's impossible for a group of people to coordinate what needs to get done without spending time on it. The larger the team, the more time is needed. As talented as we are, mind reading is not a core human competency. We need to establish common values within our team for how we make decisions and respond to problems. For managers, important processes to master include running effective meetings, future proofing against past mistakes, planning for tomorrow, and nurturing a healthy culture.

Purpose, people, process. The why, the who, and the how. A great manager constantly asks herself how she can influence these levers to improve her team's outcomes. As the team grows in size, it matters less and less how good she is personally at doing the work herself. What matters more is how much of a multiplier effect she has on her team. So how does this work in practice?

Suppose I can personally sell twenty cups of lemonade per hour.

Suppose Henry and Eliza can each sell fifteen cups of lemonade per hour.

Suppose we all worked four hours a day. Because I'm the best among us at selling lemonade, it might seem like a good use of my time to man the stand. I'd sell eighty cups a day, and Henry and

Eliza would each sell sixty cups. My contribution would be 40 percent of our total sales!

But what could I do instead with my time? Suppose I spent it teaching Henry and Eliza how to become better lemonade salespeople. (*Tell lemon jokes!* * *Portion out the ingredients ahead of time! Pour cups in bulk!*) If all this training took me thirty hours, that's the equivalent of six hundred cups of lemonade that I could have sold instead; that's a lot to give up.

And yet, if that training helps Henry and Eliza sell sixteen cups per hour instead of fifteen, it would mean an extra eight cups a day sold between the two of them. It's a small improvement, but in less than three months, they'll have made up those six hundred cups I didn't sell. If they end up working at the stand for a whole year, my thirty hours spent on training instead of personally selling lemonade will mean over two thousand extra cups sold!

Training isn't the only thing I can do. What if I used those thirty hours to recruit my neighbor Toby? He's so persuasive he could convince a leopard to buy spots.[†] Suppose my "lemonade stand on every block" vision inspires him to join the team. He ends up selling thirty cups of lemonade an hour, putting all our skills to shame. In a year, that means our stand will see an additional 21,000-plus cups sold!

If I spend all my time personally selling lemonade, then I'm contributing an *additive* amount to my business, not a multiplicative one. My performance as a manager would be considered poor because I'm actually operating as an individual contributor.

When I decided to train Henry and Eliza, my efforts resulted in slightly more lemonade output, so I had a small multiplier effect.

---

* "Why did the lemon stop rolling down the road?" "It ran out of juice."
† Also, his lemon jokes are unbelievably good. I'd share them here but he's asked me not to give away "trade secrets."

I'm on the right track, but it's nothing to write home about. When I hired Toby, it resulted in a much bigger multiplier effect.

Of course, the example above is very simple. In real life, it's not so easy to quantify what you might get out of doing one thing versus another, and we'll talk more about best practices for prioritizing your time in later chapters. But no matter what you choose, the principles of success remain the same.

Your role as a manager is not to do the work yourself, even if you are the best at it, because that will only take you so far. Your role is to improve the purpose, people, and process of your team to get as high a multiplier effect on your collective outcome as you can.

MANAGING IN SURVIVAL MODE

Investing in purpose, people, and process takes time and energy. In the lemonade stand example, I had to give up selling a few cups today because I believed that training or recruiting would set up our team to sell more lemonade down the road. Is that always the right decision? No, certainly not. Context always matters.

What if I had borrowed money to start my lemonade stand, and I needed to pay it back within two weeks or risk having to pay ten times the interest I owe? In that case, it's far more important for me to sell as much lemonade as I can myself so that my debt doesn't spiral out of control. There's not much use in planning months or years ahead if my lemonade stand is on the brink of going out of business.

Traditionally, most advice you hear about management assumes a longer time frame where if you spend a little today, you'll reap bountiful rewards in time. But that's only true if your organization isn't on fire. If it is, then all bets are off. At that point, you need to do whatever you can to extinguish the flames.

In 1943, psychologist Abraham Maslow proposed a famous

theory, known today as Maslow's hierarchy of needs, to explain human motivation. The basic idea is that certain needs trump others and you must satisfy lower-level needs before focusing on higher-level ones.

If you can't breathe, for instance, it doesn't matter if you are hungry, lonely, or unemployed. At the moment when your face starts turning blue, everything in your being will focus on how to fill your lungs with oxygen. But if you're breathing fine, it doesn't mean that life is perfect either. You're simply now able to address the next most critical barrier to your survival: getting food into your stomach.

Once you're able to breathe, your stomach is full, and you're in a safe environment, then you can focus on the next levels up in the hierarchy, such as being part of a community that supports you or contributing something meaningful with your life—what Maslow called "self-actualization."

Given that you're reading this book and wondering how you can become a better manager, it's probably safe to assume that your organization is not on the verge of imminent collapse. But if it is, then set this book down right now and figure out what you need to do to help your team turn things around. Can you rally the troops for a spectacular gambit? Can you brainstorm some MacGyver-esque tactics to get you out of your tricky bind? Can you roll up your sleeves and pitch in on making cold calls or selling glasses of lemonade?

When you are in survival mode, you do what it takes to survive.

When you're beyond survival in your team's hierarchy of needs, then you can plan for the future and think about what you can do today that will help you achieve more in the months and years ahead.

HOW DO YOU KNOW IF YOU'LL BE A GREAT MANAGER?

At this point, you know that management is the art of getting a group of people to work together to achieve better outcomes. How do you know if that's the right path for you?

Remember what I said before: great managers are made, not born. But there is one caveat, and that caveat is this: you have to *enjoy* the day-to-day of management and *want to do it*.

I once had a very talented designer on my team. She was creative and thoughtful and happened to be the most experienced person in an important product area. Everyone on her team naturally went to her for advice on big decisions. I thought to myself, *Obviously she should be a manager!* When the team expanded, I asked her if she would step up into the role. She said yes, and I gave myself a hearty pat on the back for setting her up to have even more impact.

About a year later, she quit.

I'll never forget what she told me right before she gave notice. She admitted that every morning as she lay in bed, she dreaded the prospect of going to work and managing people. As she said this, I could see that it was true. Her curious and thoughtful spark had been replaced by glassy-eyed exhaustion. Her team had issues that needed sorting through, and she was so burned out that she couldn't muster the motivation. Her everyday responsibilities were not what she was passionate about. At her core, she was a maker; she wanted long periods of uninterrupted time to go deep on a problem and create something tangible with her hands.

I learned my lesson. Ever since then, when people say they are interested in management, I try to understand what they find appealing about it and whether that matches what would be their actual day-to-day job.

Perhaps you had a great manager yourself, and you're inspired to do what she does. Perhaps you love mentoring others. Perhaps you want to progress in your career, or make more money, or call more of the shots. Some of these reasons match well with the realities of management. Some don't.

If you are wondering whether you can be a great manager, ask yourself these three questions.

Do I Find It More Motivating to Achieve a Particular Outcome or to Play a Specific Role?

As a manager, you are judged on your team's outcomes, so your job is to do whatever most helps them succeed. If your team is lacking key skills, then you need to spend your time training or hiring. If someone is creating problems for others, then you need to get him to stop. If people don't know what they should be doing, then you need to construct a plan. A lot of this work is unglamorous. But because it's important, it must be done, and if nobody else does it, then it falls to you.

This is why adaptability is a key trait of great managers. As your team changes—whether it's goals shifting, people joining or leaving, or processes evolving—what you do every day will also change. If you're committed to your purpose, then you will probably enjoy (or at least not mind) the variation that comes with the job. If, instead, there is a specific activity that you love too much to give up—whether it's seeing patients, teaching students, writing code, or designing products—then you may find your personal goals at odds with what the team needs most.

This question is more important than any other on the list, and a strong yes can make up for almost anything, which is why you see leaders with vastly different strengths and temperaments helming companies. What they have in common is that their number one priority is making their team successful, and they are willing to adapt to become the leaders that their organizations need.

Do I Like Talking with People?

You can't separate *management* from *team*, so there is no getting around the fact that, as a manager, you will have to spend a lot of time with other people. A major part of your responsibility is ensuring that the individuals you support are able to thrive. This means that listening to and talking with them are a core part of the job.

If I told you that 70 percent of your day would be spent in meetings, what's your immediate reaction? That number might be an exaggeration, but if your first thought is *No problem!* then you're the kind of person who is likely to get energy from interacting with others.

If, on the other hand, your first thought is *Wow, that sounds awful*, then you'll probably find the day-to-day of management challenging. You don't have to be an extrovert—I'm not, and plenty of other managers, from Steven Spielberg to Eleanor Roosevelt, aren't either—but the role isn't likely to suit you if what you aspire for in a workday is long, uninterrupted blocks of quiet focus.

Can I Provide Stability for an Emotionally Challenging Situation?

Because management is all about people, and each person brings his or her own unique experiences, motivations, hopes, fears, and quirks to the table, managers face their fair share of hard conversations. You may need to tell someone that she isn't meeting the expectations of her role. Even worse, you may have to look her in the eyes and tell her she no longer has a job. People may break down and tell you about the difficult issues they face that affect their work—family problems, personal tragedies, health concerns, mental illnesses, and more.

Nobody *likes* these tough situations, but some people are better than others at remaining steady and providing care and support through the bumps and dips of life. If you're the friend whom others lean on in difficult times, who might be described as empathetic and undramatic, who can be counted on to defuse rather than escalate tensions, then you'll be better equipped to deal with the range of emotionally charged scenarios that meet any manager's path.

———

Below are some other common answers to the question, "Why do you want to be a manager?" Depending on the circumstances, management may not be the best way to achieve these goals.

I Want to Progress in My Career

"Becoming a manager" is often seen as "getting a promotion," which invokes starry images of a golden future: opportunities to have more impact, take on exciting new challenges, and be rewarded with more compensation and recognition.

In many organizations, your ability to grow in your career will hit a ceiling unless you start managing people. All C-level executives lead teams. If your ambitions are to be a CEO or VP someday, you're going to need to move on to the management track. There are also jobs where, beyond a certain skill level, the only path for growth is learning how to manage and coordinate the work of more and more people—for example, in customer support or retail sales.

That said, many organizations today, particularly those that seek to attract highly skilled or creative talent, have paths for advancement that don't require managing others. For example, if you are a heart surgeon, you might hone your skills through years of practice to become a distinguished expert in your field—someone who ends up taking on the hardest cases and pioneering innovative new techniques. You shouldn't have to become a hospital general manager in order to make more money or have more impact—both expert surgeons and hospital managers are highly valued.

Similarly, in many tech companies today, roles like engineering or design offer parallel career paths once you reach a certain level of seniority—you can either grow as a manager or as an "individual contributor." Both tracks afford equal opportunities for impact, growth, and compensation up to the C-level, which means that becoming a manager is not a *promotion* but rather a *transition*. In fact, in Silicon Valley, the "10x engineer"—someone whose output is the equivalent of ten typical engineers—is so sought after that he or she commands the same pay as directors and VPs managing dozens or hundreds of people.

If you work in an organization that supports growing as an individual contributor, take advantage of the fact that you have a choice, and figure out which path is better suited to your strengths and interests.

I Want Freedom to Call the Shots

Many people dream of the day when they wake up fully in control of their own destiny. No being told what to do, no catering to anyone else's whims, no having to be told "no" or "you're wrong." They look at bosses who steer the ship through their decisions, and imagine how nice it would be to have that kind of freedom and influence.

The truth is, while managers do get to make a number of calls, those decisions must be in the interest of the team, otherwise they will lose trust and be rendered ineffective. No leader gets free rein without accountability—if their decisions turn out to be bad, they are held to task. Owners see their businesses flounder; CEOs of public companies get fired by their board.

I experienced this firsthand as a new manager during the early stages of a product proposal. As I was driving home from work one day, a brilliant idea suddenly took hold of me. It emerged fully formed in my mind—exactly what the pitch would be, how the design would work, why people would love it. Excitedly, I went home and sketched out my thoughts on paper. The next day, I called a meeting with my team. I walked the other designers through the idea and asked them to work on developing my sketch into a full proposal.

My first hint that something wasn't right was when I checked in on the work a few days later. Progress was slow. People interpreted the sketch in different ways, and hours were lost in circular debate about the proposal's core features. Thinking I hadn't explained myself well, I clarified what I was looking for. Another week passed; unfortunately, the results weren't much better.

That was when I realized the root problem: None of the designers were truly sold on my idea. They didn't think it was going to succeed. And because of that, the work trudged along, lacking heart and soul. I learned then one of my first lessons of management—the best outcomes come from inspiring people to action, not *telling* them what to do.

I Was Asked to Be a Manager

Maybe your company is turning up new hires as quickly as flowers in April. Maybe your manager now has fifteen reports and desperately needs somebody else to manage alongside her. Maybe you're seen as talented and well respected, so it feels like the next logical step. Certainly if you've been excited about management, this is a wonderful opportunity. But beware the trap of obligation. "I should" and "I can" are not sufficient reasons. Do you really want to?

This scenario is what led to me becoming a manager, and it worked out because I genuinely *enjoy* managing. It's also what drove me to ask my star designer to manage. She said yes because she was a team player who didn't want to let the team down. But the role ultimately wasn't a good fit, and we all paid the cost when she decided to leave.

If you're not sure that management is the right path for you, there are things you can do to get a better feel for it, like mentoring other folks on the team, taking on an intern, or interviewing managers who have recently transitioned to understand what their experiences were like. If you do try management and later realize that it isn't what you want to do, that's okay too. Have the honest conversation with your manager about your goals and ask her to help you explore alternative career paths.

THE DIFFERENCE BETWEEN LEADERSHIP AND MANAGEMENT

When I first started the job, I considered *manager* and *leader* to be synonyms. Managers lead, and leaders manage, right?

Nope, wrong. *Manager* is a specific role, just as *elementary school teacher* and *heart surgeon* are specific roles. As we discussed a few pages ago, there are clear principles outlining what a manager does and how his success is measured.

Leadership, on the other hand, is the particular skill of being able to guide and influence other people.

"What makes a good leader is that they eschew the spotlight in favor of spending time and energy to do what they need to do to support and protect their people," writes Simon Sinek in *Leaders Eat Last*. In return, "We offer our blood and sweat and tears and do everything we can to see our leader's vision come to life."

Now, a manager who doesn't know how to influence others isn't going to be particularly effective at improving the outcomes of her team. So to be a great manager, one must certainly be a leader.

A leader, on the other hand, doesn't have to be a manager. Anyone can exhibit leadership, regardless of their role. Think of a store clerk calmly directing shoppers to safety when the screeching tornado bell goes off in a mall. Think of a passionate citizen going door-to-door and convincing neighbors to join him in protesting a recent decision. Think of generations upon generations of mothers and fathers demonstrating to their children what it means to act like a responsible adult.

If you picture your own organization, you can probably come up with many examples of leadership: an individual contributor who surfaces important customer complaints and then coordinates solutions across multiple teams, a team member who rallies a group to work on a new idea, a veteran employee who is a sought-out oracle of wisdom. If you can pinpoint a problem and motivate others to work with you to solve it, then you're leading.

Leadership is a quality rather than a job. We are all leaders and followers at different points in our lives. Many aspects of this book should be useful to those looking to grow as leaders as well as managers, and great managers should cultivate leadership not just in themselves but also within their teams.

This is an important distinction because while the role of a manager can be given to someone (or taken away), leadership is not something that can be bestowed. It must be earned. People must *want* to follow you.

You can be someone's manager, but if that person does not

trust or respect you, you will have limited ability to influence him. I did not suddenly become a "leader" the day my title officially changed. On the contrary, some of my reports were initially skeptical, and it took time for us to develop a strong relationship.

In your early days as a manager, what matters most is transitioning gracefully into the role and nailing the essentials of leading a small team. Only when you have built trust with your reports will you have the credibility to help them achieve more together.

Chapter Two

Your First Three Months

AVOID

ASPIRE

Whenever a new manager joins my team, my favorite questions to ask a few months in are: "What turned out to be more challenging than you expected, and what was easier than you expected?"

For the first question, one manager laughed and quoted me a poster on our walls: "Every day feels like a week." His answer was a variation on the most common thing I hear—*there's so much to learn and you feel overwhelmed.*

As for what turned out to be easier than expected, the answers were more varied. An individual contributor turned manager told me how glad he was that he already knew everyone on his team and what they were working on. A manager new to the company shared how helpful her peers were in answering her "n00b-ish" questions.

No matter how you've arrived at your new role, congratulations are in order because this much is true: Somebody—more likely *many* people—believed in you and your potential to lead a team. That's why you're holding this book.

Your path here probably took one of the four routes below:

- **Apprentice:** Your manager's team is growing, so you've been asked to manage a part of it going forward.
- **Pioneer:** You are a founding member of a new group, and you're now responsible for its growth.
- **New Boss:** You're coming in to manage an already established

team, either within your existing organization or at a new one.

- **Successor:** Your manager has decided to leave, and you are taking his place.

Depending on your path, different things may be easy or hard for you in your first three months. Choose your own adventure below to learn more about what to expect.

THE APPRENTICE

As teams grow, so do opportunities for new managers. I went down this path when our team's leader, Rebekah, realized that we needed more support after our team doubled.

What to Take Advantage Of

This is usually the easiest way to transition into being a manager. Because your own manager has been looking over the team and knows everyone involved, you'll typically have more guidance than in the other transition scenarios.

When I started, Rebekah gave me a list of names and said, "Here's who I think should be on your team." In hindsight, I can see just how intentional she was in planning my transition. She started me off with just a handful of reports whom she felt I could successfully manage, and she worked to ensure I was set up well (including helping me get to a great relationship with my initially skeptical report from that first 1:1).

In my first few months, Rebekah was my constant sounding board. If I wasn't sure how to respond to a request or if a situation came up that I felt unprepared for, she was there to coach me. If you're transitioning as an apprentice, work with your manager on a joint plan for getting started. Questions to discuss include:

- What will be my scope to start, and how do you expect it to change over time?
- How will my transition be communicated?
- What do I need to know about the people that I'll be managing?
- What important team goals or processes should I be aware of and help push forward?
- What does success look like in my first three and six months?
- How can the two of us stay aligned on who does what?

You have a sense of what works and what doesn't. Because you've gotten a front-row view into how your team operates—how meetings are run, how decisions get made, what your team members are like—you're coming into your role with considerable information.

A useful exercise to go through at the beginning of your transition is to sit down and make a list of all the things that are awesome about the current state of the world. Does everyone get along? Are your processes efficient? Is your team known for rigorous and high-quality work?

Now, next to that, create a list of all the things that could be better. Is your team cagey about deadlines? Does it seem like priorities are always shifting? Is there that one really long weekly meeting nobody wants to attend?

These two lists give you the start of a plan for what you should and shouldn't change. You don't need to fix what isn't broken, but neither should you feel like you're stuck in a time machine of *this is how it was always done*. After all, that's why you got the job! Taking the time to reflect on the biggest opportunities for improvement helps you understand how to best act as a multiplier for your team.

You're able to ramp up quickly because you have context. Unlike a manager coming in from the outside, you have a good understanding of the team already—not just how it works but also its goals and the projects that are in flight. Because of this, you don't need as long of a period to listen and learn. You can start being useful much faster.

What to Watch Out For

It can feel awkward to establish a new dynamic with former peers. Before, you were just another individual contributor on the team. Now, you are the boss, which means your relationship with teammates might feel altered. When I started, I found the below challenging, especially with reports whom I considered friends:

Playing the role of coach: Your job now includes understanding your former peers' career goals, what kinds of projects are well suited to their strengths and interests, what they need help with, and how they are doing relative to expectations. At first, it felt strange and sometimes uncomfortable asking a friend or former peer, "What do you want to be working toward in a year's time?" or "What do you consider your strengths?" especially when we didn't talk about those things before.

But don't avoid those conversations, even if they feel awkward. Seek to understand what your new reports care about. Give them feedback about what they're doing well and where they might stretch (covered in a later chapter). Think of yourself as a coach who is there to support and help your people reach their goals.

Having hard conversations: When I gave my peers feedback on their work in the past, I'd frame criticisms as suggestions— "Hey, just an idea, but have you considered . . . ?" I knew that, ultimately, they owned their own decisions. When I became my peers' manager, I found it difficult to change this mindset even when I needed to.

The manager–report relationship is different than the peer relationship. You are now responsible for the outcome of your team, including all the decisions that are made within it. If something is getting in the way of great work happening, you need to address it swiftly and directly. This may mean giving people difficult feedback or making some hard calls. The sooner you internalize that you own the outcomes of your team, the easier it becomes to have these conversations.

Having people treat you differently or share less information with you: I was surprised when my peers, who used to be so transparent with me about everything, suddenly seemed to share less after I became their manager. They wouldn't always tell me when they were struggling or annoyed or had a disagreement with another member of the team. If I walked in on two of them venting about something, they'd stop and look at me sheepishly. I found it harder to get a clear picture of what was happening on the ground.

Over time, however, I recognized that, yes, this was normal. My reports were wary of bothering me or coming across poorly. It was up to me to work harder to establish a trusting relationship (the topic of the next chapter).

It's tricky to balance your individual contributor commitments with management. As an apprentice, you rarely start out with a big team. It's more likely that you begin with a handful of reports and welcome more people in over time. This means that, in the early days, most new apprentice managers are also handling individual contributor responsibilities. In addition to supporting others, you're also still selling lemonade.

I thought this was a fine arrangement. I was afraid that if I stopped doing design work myself, I'd slowly lose my skills, which would make it harder for me to be an effective leader. Unfortunately, the mistake that I made—and that I see virtually every apprentice manager make—is continuing to do individual contributor work past the point at which it is sustainable.

When my team became six or so, I was still the lead designer for a complex project that demanded many hours of the week. Because my management responsibilities were also growing, every time something out of the ordinary happened—a report needed extra one-on-one attention or our team had multiple reviews to prepare for that week—I wouldn't have enough time to devote to my own project. The quality of my work suffered, my peers got frustrated, and the balls I was desperately trying to juggle plopped to the ground.

I finally realized that I had to give up wanting to be both a design manager *and* a designer, because in attempting to do both, I was doing neither well. Don't learn this the hard way—at the point in which your team becomes four or five people, you should have a plan for how to scale back your individual contributor responsibilities so that you can be the best manager for your people.

THE PIONEER

You were among the first to take on a challenge that is now turning into a bigger team effort. Growth is a sign that things are going well, so take pride in what you've accomplished! You might be a start-up founder going from three people in a garage to ten full-time employees, or the first accountant hired into an organization that's now building out an entire finance department. As you grow your team, keep in mind the following.

What to Take Advantage Of

You've done the job, so you know what it takes. You were the first, the original, the alpha; no one knows better than you what the job entails because you helped define it. Now it's time to take it to the next level.

To be successful, you'll need to unearth all the values and know-how in your head and pass them along to others. In the early days, make sure that you're spending time calibrating with your new team on what your group's goals, values, and processes ought to be. Some questions to ask yourself in preparation:

* How do I make decisions?
* What do I consider a job well done?
* What are all the responsibilities I took care of when it was just me?
* What's easy or hard about working in this function?
* What new processes are needed now that this team is growing?

You get to build the team that you want. One of the privileges of being a pioneer is that you're able to choose the people you want to work with and how you want to work with them. Instead of inheriting a team, you get to create a brand-new one. Be deliberate about the people and culture you're setting up, and ask yourself:

* What qualities do I want in a team member?
* What skills does our team need to complement my own?

- How should this team look and function in a year?
- How will my own role and responsibilities evolve?

What to Watch Out For

You may not have much support. The life of a pioneer is filled with adventure and solitude. Think of the first designer at a company being asked to grow the user-experience discipline. Whom does she turn to if she has questions about how to hire and on-board other designers? She's the only one of her kind! As a pioneer, you continually find yourself alone in new, unfamiliar terrain. But that doesn't mean you can't seek out help.

Though you may be the only manager doing what you do at your organization, there are two other groups you can lean on for support: other managers in your organization who support related functions, and managers in your area of expertise outside your organization.

At Facebook, the engineering team was always many times bigger than design. Whenever I encountered a new challenge—our weekly team meeting became inefficient, for example, or my reports were asking for clearer career paths—I'd turn to my manager friends in engineering and ask them if they ever dealt with something similar. Eight times out of ten, the answer was, "Of course, we had that problem three years ago when we were your size, and here's what we learned."

Outside of your organization, finding a group of leaders in similar roles at other places can provide you with an invaluable network of support. My friend who is an entrepreneur swears by what he calls "informal CEO training" from casual dinners he attends with other founders. For me, I'll often have coffee with design managers from other companies like Google, Airbnb, and Amazon, where we'll discuss common challenges in the design industry or bigger trends we're seeing. Though we keep away from discussing the specifics of our work, being able to talk shop with others who get what I do always teaches me a lot.

It's tricky to balance your IC work with management. *See description from "The Apprentice," pages 43–44.*

THE NEW BOSS

A team is welcoming you as its new leader, which is no small achievement! If you find yourself in this situation, you probably have past management experience. Organizations rarely hire untested managers to oversee already established teams. Assuming that the job isn't completely new to you, there are still some nuances to be aware of.

What to Take Advantage Of

People cut you slack in the beginning. The biggest advantage of being new is that you have a window of time, usually about three months, when everyone recognizes that you're the new kid on the block. You are not expected to know anything at first, from what everyone works on to what the current strategy is. Mistakes you make will be brushed aside, and you'll find that your colleagues are usually quite willing to help you get up to speed. Use the newbie card to your advantage by asking as many questions of as many people as you can. You might feel the urge to keep quiet and not draw any attention to yourself until you "know enough," but if your goal is to ramp up quickly, you need to be proactive in your onboarding.

If you anticipate needing to work closely with someone, see if that person would be willing to meet one-on-one with you so you can get to know each other and understand what she cares about. If you're not sure whom you'll be working with, ask your manager for a list of people to reach out to.

Don't shy away from asking questions, even if you believe you're the only one who doesn't know. (*New person question, but what does the acronym IC stand for?**) Sometimes, these questions also help others. During a particularly active discussion around a go-to-market plan, a new manager on my team once piped up, "Excuse me—I'm new, so pardon the question—but can someone please explain what we're hoping to achieve with this launch?"

That question led the room to stop and take a step back. Having gotten so caught up in the launch details, we realized we needed to make sure we were all aligned on the broader goal first. At the end of the discussion, a long-tenured team member said admiringly to the new manager, "*I* hadn't even connected the dots on what we cared about, so your question was awesome."

You start with a blank slate. Did you have a reputation for being indecisive or stubborn in your last role? Now that you're coming in fresh, you have a chance to form new ties and reset your identity.

This also works the other way around. Some of your reports will appreciate the chance to build the kind of manager–report relationship that they've always wanted. Stay open-minded and curious as you meet everyone.

A new boss friend of mine was told by a colleague that one of her reports was "a worse-than-average employee." She thanked the colleague for the information but resolved to come to her own conclusions. Over the next six months, she grew to develop a fantastic relationship with that report, who thrived under her coaching—within a year, that person was promoted to be a team lead.

To make the most of having a blank slate, give everyone the benefit of the doubt, no matter what you're told. Hopefully others will do the same for you. And be up front with people—especially

---

* "Individual contributor"

your reports—about the kind of relationship you'd like to build and the kind of manager you want to be. These topics are easier to discuss up front before you've settled into patterns and routines. In your first few one-on-one meetings, ask your reports the following questions to understand what their "dream manager" looks like.

- What did you and your past manager discuss that was most helpful to you?
- What are the ways in which you'd like to be supported?
- How do you like to be recognized for great work?
- What kind of feedback is most useful for you?
- Imagine that you and I had an amazing relationship. What would that look like?

What to Watch Out For

It takes a while to adjust to the norms of a new environment. No matter how talented you are, learning how a new team works takes time, whether you're joining a different company or changing roles at an existing company. One of the biggest mistakes new bosses make is thinking they need to jump in and exert their opinions right away to show that they are capable.

Actually, that approach tends to backfire. Few things are more annoying than a new person wasting everyone else's time because they are trying to prove they know something when their opinion isn't actually informed.

In your first few months, your primary job is to listen, ask questions, and learn. New managers on my team tell me that the thing they most want to understand is how to calibrate their expectations around "what's normal." One effective way to do that is to look at specific scenarios together with your own manager. Questions to ask include:

- What does it mean to do a great job versus an average or poor job? Can you give me some examples?
- Can you share your impressions of how you think Project X or Meeting Y went? Why do you think that?
- I noticed that Z happened the other day. . . . Is that normal or should I be concerned?
- What keeps you up at night? Why?
- How do you determine which things to prioritize?

You need to invest in building new relationships. As a new boss with a new team, you're back to square one when it comes to establishing trust. Besides the many names and faces to keep track of, you might feel the isolation of being an outsider. Your teammates all know each other, whereas you don't yet have that same level of comfort with the group. It can be especially challenging if you feel that people aren't being completely open with you.

One tactic a friend of mine uses to buck this trend is to address the elephant in the room: "Since I'm new, you might not feel comfortable sharing everything with me right away. I hope to earn your trust over time. I'll start by sharing more about myself, including my biggest failure ever . . ." I love this anecdote because it's the epitome of "show, don't tell." What better way to set the tone that it's okay to talk about anything than by diving head-first into revealing a personal vulnerability?

Building a great relationship doesn't happen overnight. In the next chapter, we'll go much deeper into the ingredients needed for trust.

You don't know the job and what it takes. When you said yes to the role, you couldn't have predicted the exact nature of the team, the work, and the environment. Now that you're here, maybe the job and its challenges aren't exactly what you envisioned.

In this situation, the best policy is to be honest with your own manager about what's working for you and what isn't, and to understand his expectations for your ramp up. A new manager on my team once confided in me that he'd had more difficulties connecting with his peers than he expected, and as a result he wasn't able to influence decision-making.

Because he brought it up proactively, we were able to create a plan for him to have some honest conversations with his partners. They immediately put in extra effort to include him in discussions once they heard his concerns, while also sharing with him some valuable feedback on how he could communicate more effectively. Within a week, the situation turned around, and his ramp up went much smoother after that.

THE SUCCESSOR

The successor transition is like the apprentice's but with a twist: because your manager is leaving, you're taking on supporting the entire team yourself, not just a portion of it. Though most successors have prior management experience, it's still a significant increase in responsibility and you may feel you have big shoes to fill.

While the advantages of this transition are similar to those of the apprentice (you have a sense of what works and what doesn't, and you're able to ramp up quickly because you come in with context, as described earlier), the differences are also striking.

What to Watch Out For

It can feel awkward to establish a new dynamic with former peers. See description from "The Apprentice," pages 43–44.

The increase in responsibility can feel overwhelming. It's not unusual to go through periods of feeling that you bit off more than you can chew. After all, you're now being asked to do your former boss's job. And despite having a sense of what that entails, most successors are surprised by the extent of what they've inherited. "I had no idea the lengths my former manager went to to shield us from the many requests from other teams," a colleague told me in amazement after she became the successor. "I'm getting contacted left and right every day, and I realize now how much work he did behind the scenes to take care of things."

Don't be too hard on yourself, and ask for support from your new manager as well as others around you (more on that in Chapter Five: Managing Yourself). It's also helpful to be up front with your colleagues that they should expect a period of transition as you ramp up. One friend shared his most repeated line in those early weeks: "Our last manager left big shoes to fill, and while I'll do my best, I expect I'll go through a few bumps along the way. I want to ask you for your help and support during this period." Setting the stage explicitly like that lets others understand what you're going through and offer aid as you adjust to your new scope.

You feel pressure to do things exactly like your former manager. Because the memory of how things used to be is still fresh in your team's mind, it's easy to fall into the trap of thinking you need to preserve the status quo. You may feel as if everyone is looking to you to be just as good at everything as your former manager, even though you're different people.

Change is a prerequisite for improvement, so give yourself permission to move on from the past. Remember the well-known adage: "Be yourself; everyone else is already taken." You will be far more successful aspiring to be the leader *you* want to be and playing to *your* strengths than trying to live up to some other ideal.

When a beloved manager on my team, Robyn Morris, left after many years to pursue a different passion, I was talking with one of his successors about how much we all missed him and deeply felt his absence.

She said to me, "No one person can entirely replace Robyn, and that's okay. More of us will just need to step up to grow into the gaps that he left behind." Sure enough, a year later, the team was thriving, and the ways that this manager and others blossomed as leaders have been amazing to watch.

———

Your first three months as a new manager are a time of incredible transition. By the end of it, the day-to-day starts to feel familiar—you're adapting to new routines, you're investing in new relationships, and you may begin to have a sense of how you can best support your team.

But time isn't a substitute for comfort. That new-kid-at-school feeling may linger for months or years longer. New managers often ask me, "How long will it take to feel like I know what I'm doing?" I reply quite honestly, "It took me about three years."

In the chapters ahead, we'll look at all the major aspects of a manager's job—from coaching reports to hiring new ones, from organizing meetings to organizing the anxiety inside your head. Hand in hand with the experience of actually *doing*, the goal of these upcoming stories, principles, and exercises is to take you from your first ninety days and make you into the manager you want to be.

Chapter Three

Leading a Small Team

AVOID

ASPIRE

When I had around eight people on my team, we would run a weekly meeting called critique.

Even though this meeting was ninety minutes long, it was one of my favorite parts of the week. The team would gather around a conference room table with a giant TV. We'd pick an order—clockwise or counterclockwise—and someone would volunteer to go first. After fiddling with cables and plugging in her laptop, the presenter's latest work would pop up on the screen before us.

While the designer described the problem she was trying to solve and how she got to her present solution, our eyes drank in the details of this potential blueprint for the future. We imagined ourselves as typical users waking up one morning and being presented with this new experience. What did we notice first? What was clear or confusing? What would make this even better?

After her brief introduction, the critiques would start. Anybody in the room could chime in with questions, concerns, or suggestions. These could be as strategic as "Does the problem being solved here really matter?" or as tactical as "Should the collection of items be displayed as a grid or a list?"

The team would discuss and debate. We'd offer up new ideas to explore in the spirit of making the experience better. We'd bring up similar examples to learn from. We'd connect the dots on projects that different designers were working on. At its best, critique was honest, creative, and deeply collaborative. At the end, the presenter would emerge with a list of clear next steps. We'd move on to the next designer, and the process would repeat until everyone had a chance to present and get feedback.

To me, this meeting always felt like the epitome of what I loved about managing a small team. You don't build Rome in a day, and you don't start off your management career standing in front of a packed room delivering a ten-year vision. Instead, most of us begin by managing just a few people. You cultivate an environment of trust while diving into the detailed depths of the work. Everybody knows everybody, and two pizzas are enough to feed the group.

Managing a small team is about mastering a few basic fundamentals: developing a healthy manager–report relationship and creating an environment of support. In this chapter, we'll dive in to the specifics of those skills.

EVERYTHING ALWAYS GOES BACK TO PEOPLE

Remember our definition of management? A manager's job is to *get better outcomes from a group of people working together* through influencing purpose, people, and process.

With a small team, maintaining a shared sense of purpose is straightforward. You don't get many crossed wires when your team can still fit around one table. That leaves people and process to focus on. Of those two, people are by far the most important.

What leads people to do great work? It feels like a complicated question but it really isn't, as Andy Grove points out in his classic *High Output Management*. He flips the question around and asks: What gets in the way of good work? There are only two possibilities. The first is that *people don't know how to do good work*. The second is that they know how, but *they aren't motivated*.

Let's go one step further. Why would someone not know how to do great work? The obvious answer is that she might not have the right skills for the job. If you needed your house painted and you hired an accountant, you shouldn't be surprised if the paint job is splotchy. Someone trained in bookkeeping doesn't necessarily have the right experience to be a first-rate painter. As the manager, you can do one of two things here: help your report learn those skills or hire somebody else with the skills you need.

Why would someone not be motivated to do great work? One possible answer is that he doesn't have a clear picture of what great work looks like. Another possibility is that the role doesn't speak to his aspirations; he *can*, but he'd rather be doing something else. Or perhaps he thinks nothing will change if he puts in more effort—there will be no rewards if things improve, and no penalties if they don't, so why bother?

The first step to addressing any concerns about lackluster work is diagnosing the people issues behind it. Is it a matter of motivation or skill? This doesn't have to be complicated. You can understand this through a series of conversations with your report. First, discuss whether your expectations are aligned—does "great work" mean the same thing for both of you? Then discuss whether it's a matter of motivation. If both of those don't resolve your concerns, then dive in to whether the issue is with skills.

Of course, the above only works if you can have honest, constructive conversations together. No matter the work you do or the size of your team, knowing how to diagnose and solve problems with your reports is critical to your shared success. That starts first and foremost with building a stable foundation for your relationship.

TRUST IS THE MOST IMPORTANT INGREDIENT

"You must trust people, or life becomes impossible," the writer Anton Chekhov once said. This is true of all relationships—friendships, marriages, partnerships—and the manager–report relationship is no different.

Sounds obvious, right? But it is easier said than done, especially when you're the one holding more of the chips at the table. No matter how you slice it, you are your reports' boss. You have more impact on their day-to-day than they have on yours. This means that the responsibility of building a trusting relationship lies more with you than with them.

Think of your relationship with your own manager. When things aren't going well and you shuffle into her office feeling discouraged or overwhelmed, what do you say?

If you're like I was in my first few years, the answer is: nothing. I wasn't comfortable admitting to my manager that I was struggling. I didn't want her to think that she misplaced her faith in me. If one of the projects I was working on was going off the rails because I had too much on my plate, I'd paint it as "I'm juggling a lot right now, but no need to worry, I'll be fine." Meanwhile, my stress level would shoot up to eleven out of ten as I worked madly around the clock.

It's human nature to want your manager to think well of you. Coming across as a complainer, a failure, or a problem employee seems like one of those obvious don'ts in managing up.

The issue, of course, is that if your reports don't tell you how they're really feeling, you can't help them. You may miss early warning signs that lead to bigger problems down the road. People's dissatisfaction will fester beneath the surface until one day they surprise you with their resignation. And most of the time when that happens, they're not just quitting your company, they are also quitting you.

You can avoid being blindsided by developing a relationship founded on trust, in which your reports feel that they can be completely honest with you because they have no doubt that you truly care about them. You've accomplished this if the following three statements are true.

My reports regularly bring their biggest challenges to my attention. A hallmark of a trusting relationship is that people feel they can share their mistakes, challenges, and fears with you. If they're struggling through an assignment, they tell you right away so you can work through it together. If they're having issues collaborating with somebody, you hear it first from them and not through the grapevine. If something's keeping them up at night, they tell you what it is.

One of my teammates shared with me a simple litmus test for assessing the health of her relationships: If she asks her report how things are going and the answer for multiple weeks is "Everything is fine," she takes it as a sign to prod further. It's much more likely that the report is shy about getting into the gory details than that everything is consistently rainbows and butterflies.

My report and I regularly give each other critical feedback and it isn't taken personally. If your report does work that you don't think is great, are you comfortable saying that directly? Similarly, would your report tell you if he thinks you've made a mistake?

My friend Mark Rabkin shared a tip with me that I love: strive for all your one-on-one meetings to feel a little awkward. Why? Because the most important and meaningful conversations have that characteristic. It isn't easy to discuss mistakes, confront tensions, or talk about deep fears or secret hopes, but no strong relationship can be built on superficial pleasantries alone.

There's no wordsmithery that gets around the awkwardness of expressing a sentiment like, "I don't feel that you recognize when I'm doing a good job" or "Last week, when you said X, it made me feel as if you don't really understand my project." But these things need to be said in order to be addressed, and with a bedrock of trust, the conversations become easier.

Imagine you go shopping with your best friend and she comes out in an unflattering green-and-yellow sweater. "How do I look?" she asks you.

"Like a caterpillar," you say. You're not worried about insulting her because she's your best friend and she'll know you said it out of affection rather than spite.

You'd think twice about directing that same line toward a stranger because you don't have any shared history and you might offend them. It takes repeated good experiences to build up to a level of trust where you can be vulnerable and compassionately critical with each other. In the next chapter, we'll talk more about how to give feedback well.

My reports would gladly work for me again. One of the truest indicators of the strength of your relationships is whether your reports would want you as their manager in the future if they were given the choice. When you see a manager taking on a new role and members of his former team also make the leap with him, that says a lot about his leadership.

In anonymous surveys to track team health, some companies explicitly ask the question, "Would you work for your manager again?" If your organization doesn't do this, simply reflecting on the question can be useful.

For each report, can you say with confidence that he or she would want to be on your team again? If you aren't sure that the answer is yes, it's probably no (much like how if you have to ask, "Am I in love?" you're probably not).

You can also get an approximate reading by asking your report, "What are the qualities of a perfect manager for you?" and evaluating how you compare to the description you get back. (Asking directly, "Would you work for me again?" definitely clears the bar of being awkward but doesn't set you up well to receive completely honest responses.)

STRIVE TO BE HUMAN, NOT A BOSS

I once shared some critical feedback with one of my reports who was also a manager. Even though he was quite talented, I gathered from his team that he had a tendency to micromanage. His reports wanted to see him work *through* them rather than dictate the details of their day-to-day.

As I relayed this, I saw my report deflate. I imagined him kicking himself as his mind raced through all the interactions he'd had in the past few weeks, wondering what specific things he'd said that made people feel this way.

I could understand how he felt because I had gotten the exact same feedback before. He started to tell me what he thought had happened and what he might have overlooked. "I feel you," I replied. He paused like I had said something profound. "You do?" he asked. "Yeah. I struggle with it too," I said.

I then shared an example from just the day before, when I hadn't done a good job walking the line between giving actionable feedback and micromanaging the details. My report looked relieved by the end of my story. "Thank you for that," he said. "It was incredibly helpful."

His reaction surprised me because, as far as I knew, I hadn't said anything useful. We hadn't discussed any specific tactics to address the problem. All I did was admit that I had basically the same issue.

But the learning stuck with me because what spoke to him wasn't the fact that I had rattled off a bunch of amazing advice. It was that, for a moment, we related. I wasn't some authority figure but rather another person also wading through the choppy waters of management. That helped us connect as individuals, and going forward, it was easier for us to discuss pretty much anything else.

The way to earn trust with your reports is no different than how you earn it with anyone else, and requires the following few actions.

Respect and Care about Your Report

A few years ago, I attended a management workshop led by a senior executive who had an amazing track record as a manager: In his long tenure, nobody reporting to him had ever quit to take a competing offer. What was his secret? "If you take nothing else away from today," he told us, "remember this: *managing is caring.*"

If you don't truly respect or care about your report, there is no faking it. Trust me, they know. None of us are such brilliant actors that we can control the thousands of tiny signals we are subconsciously sending through our body language. If you don't believe in your heart of hearts that someone can succeed, it will be impossible for you to convey your strong belief in them.

There are a few nuances here. When I was a new manager, I thought that caring about my report meant supporting her side of the story whenever there was a disagreement. When others gave her critical feedback, I thought it was my job to jump to her defense to show that I had her back.

As it turns out, supporting and caring for someone doesn't mean always agreeing with them or making excuses for their mistakes. The people in my life who have been most invested in helping me succeed—folks like my parents, best friends, and managers—are often also the ones who most readily tell me why they think I'm wrong. (My mom likes to remind me that despite repeated tantrums where I insisted on eating ice cream for breakfast every morning as a kid, her steadfast refusal is the reason I have healthy eating habits today.)

What caring does mean, however, is doing your best to help your report be successful and fulfilled in her work. It means taking the time to learn what she cares about. It means understanding that we are not separate people at work and at home—sometimes the personal blends into the professional, and that's okay.

Another nuance of respect is that it must be unconditional because it's about *the person as a whole* rather than what she does for you. I've never encountered a manager who wasn't a bastion of support for individuals they considered top performers. It's easy to like and have a great relationship with someone who is kicking ass. The harder test is, what happens when she struggles?

If your report feels that your support and respect are based on her performance, then it will be hard for her to be honest with you when things are rocky. If, on the other hand, she feels that you care about her *no matter what*, and nothing can change that—not even failure—then you will get honesty in return.

I know people who have been let go by their managers and still make time to see them for lunch and catch up on life. We are more than the output of our work on a particular team at a particular moment in time, and true respect reflects that.

Invest Time to Help Your Report

The most precious resource you have is your own time and energy, and when you spend it on your team, it goes a long way toward building healthy relationships. This is why one-on-one meetings ("1:1s" for short) are such an important part of management. I recommend no less than a weekly 1:1 with every report for thirty minutes, and more time if needed.

Even if you sit next to someone and see him every day, 1:1s let you discuss topics that may never come up otherwise—for example, what motivates him, what his long-term career aspirations are, how he's generally feeling about his work, and more. One-on-ones should be focused on your report and what would help him be more successful, not on you and what you need. If you're looking for a status update, use another channel. Rare one-on-one face time is better spent on topics that are harder to discuss in a group or over email.

The ideal 1:1 leaves your report feeling that it was useful for her. If she thinks that the conversation was pleasant but largely unmemorable, then you can do better. Remember that your job is to be a multiplier for your people. If you can remove a barrier, provide a valuable new perspective, or increase their confidence, then you're enabling them to be more successful.

How can you achieve stellar 1:1s? The answer is preparation. It's rare that an amazing conversation springs forth when nobody has a plan for what to talk about. I tell my reports that I want our time together to be valuable, so we should focus on what's most important for them. Here are some ideas to get started:

- **Discuss top priorities:** What are the one, two, or three most critical outcomes for your report and how can you help her tackle these challenges?

- **Calibrate what "great" looks like:** Do you have a shared vision of what you're working toward? Are you in sync about goals or expectations?

- **Share feedback:** What feedback can you give that will help your report, and what can your report tell you that will make you more effective as a manager?

- **Reflect on how things are going:** Once in a while, it's useful to zoom out and talk about your report's general state of mind—how is he feeling on the whole? What's making him satisfied or dissatisfied? Have any of his goals changed? What has he learned recently and what does he want to learn going forward?

It's helpful for both manager and report to think through the topics they want to bring to the 1:1 conversation. Every morning, I've gotten into the habit of scanning my calendar and compiling a list of questions for each person I'm meeting with.

Why questions? Because a coach's best tool for understanding what's going on is to *ask*. Don't presume you know what the problem or solution is. Too often, attempts to "help" aren't actually helpful, even when served with the best of intentions. We all remember lectures that went in one ear and out the other because it was obvious the other party didn't understand our real problem, or when unasked-for "help" feels indistinguishable from micromanaging or meddling.

Your job as a manager isn't to dole out advice or "save the day"—it's to empower your report to find the answer herself. She has more context than you on the problems she's dealing with, so she's in the best position to uncover the solution. Let her lead the 1:1 while you listen and probe.

Here are some of my favorite questions to get the conversation moving:

- **Identify:** These questions focus on what really matters for your report and what topics are worth spending more time on.

    What's top of mind for you right now?

    What priorities are you thinking about this week?

    What's the best use of our time today?

- **Understand:** Once you've identified a topic to discuss, these next questions get at the root of the problem and what can be done about it.

    What does your ideal outcome look like?

    What's hard for you in getting to that outcome?

    What do you really care about?

    What do you think is the best course of action?

    What's the worst-case scenario you're worried about?

- **Support:** These questions zero in on how you can be of greatest service to your report.

    How can I help you?

    What can I do to make you more successful?

    What was the most useful part of our conversation today?

Be Honest and Transparent about Your Report's Performance

As a manager, your perspective on how your report is doing carries far more weight than his perspective on how you are doing. After all, you're the one who determines what he works on and whether he should get a promotion or be fired.

This power imbalance means that the responsibility falls to you to be honest and transparent when it comes to how you are evaluating performance.

Your report should have a clear sense at all times of what your expectations are and where he stands. If he is often wondering, *What does my manager think of me?* then you need to dial up your level of feedback. Don't assume he can read between the lines or that no news is good news. If you think he is the epitome of awesome, tell him. If you don't think he is operating at the level you'd like to see, he should know that, too, and precisely why you feel that way. For specifics on how to master the art of giving feedback, see the next chapter.

Admit Your Own Mistakes and Growth Areas

No one is perfect, and managers are no exception. You will make mistakes. You will let people down. You will have moments where you say the wrong thing and make the situation worse rather than better. When that happens, don't fall into the trap of thinking that because you're the boss, you can't admit your shortcomings or weaknesses. Instead, apologize. Admit that you screwed up, and take meaningful action to do better in the future.

A while ago, a well-respected manager I worked with sent a broadly distributed note that implied a particular team wasn't working fast enough. The frustration in his tone was obvious, and because of his seniority, the note had a demoralizing effect. Someone informed him in private that he was missing important context on how the team was operating, and that the tone of his note wasn't helping. Immediately, he followed up with a sincere apology.

People will forget what you said, people will forget what you did, but people will never forget how you made them feel, goes the popular saying. I've forgotten the specifics of that email, but I still remember the difference that apology made.

When we are going through tough times, the thing that's often the most helpful isn't advice or answers but empathy. This wasn't intuitive to me at first because I assumed that leaders always showed up with confidence and know-how. I figured I should act like I knew what to do in front of my reports, even when I didn't feel that way.

Brené Brown, research expert in courage, shame, and empathy, begs to differ. She proposes that there is enormous power in expressing vulnerability: "Vulnerability sounds like truth and feels like courage. Truth and courage aren't always comfortable, but they're never weakness."

These days, I try to admit when I don't have the answers or when I'm working through my own personal challenges. I'll say things like the following:

- "I don't know the answer. What do you think?"
- "I want to come clean and apologize for what I did/said the other day. . . ."
- "One of my personal growth areas this half is . . ."
- "I'm afraid I don't know enough to help you with that problem. Here's someone you should talk to instead. . . ."

I've found that by showing up authentically, with my fears, mistakes, and uncertainties out in the open rather than swept under the rug, I've been able to build better relationships with my reports.

HELP PEOPLE PLAY TO THEIR STRENGTHS

A few years ago, I found myself having a difficult conversation with my manager Chris about the design of a new product we were building. He had repeatedly given me feedback that what he'd seen in the past few reviews felt too complicated.

He was right. My diagnosis was that we were simultaneously moving too quickly and trying to add too many bells and whistles. The result was that the entire experience felt confusing. However, I was struggling to get everyone aligned on cutting features and pushing back our release date.

I remember staring at a blank spot on the wall, feeling dejected. Chris was quiet for a moment, and then said: "Remember that you have good values."

To this day, it's hard to describe the power those simple words had. He could have said dozens of other things to make me feel better—"You'll find a way through this," "It's not as bad as you think," or "Here are some things to try." But what he said instead was specific to *me*, and something I felt he genuinely believed. It didn't mean my opinions were always right, but his vote of confidence that they came from a principled place restored some of the confidence I had lost. By recognizing a strength of mine, Chris gave me a renewed sense of motivation.

In the years since, I've called to mind the phrase *you have good values* many, many times—when I wondered if I should share a contrarian opinion, when I was facing strong pushback on a proposal, when I debated taking on a new challenge.

We humans are wired to see the bad more clearly than the good. It's an evolutionary advantage, after all. Imagine you are an ancient cave dweller surveying the landscape: Would you rather be better at noticing what's fine and normal—deer grazing, tree branches swaying, the sun shining—or at spotting the hungry lion in the shadows?

Whenever I used to read my manager's feedback, I'd give the strengths and "going well" section a passing glance and focus primarily on the "areas for improvement." If I had a highly productive day but I bombed one meeting, guess what would be on my mind as I was driving home?

As a manager, my attention is similarly drawn toward the problem spots. I'm usually focused on the designs that aren't quite there, the projects that are slipping behind schedule, or the teams that have hiring needs. Whenever I'm talking with my reports, it's easy to spend all our time on the things that need improvement.

And yet, all of us likely remember moments when a kind word about our unique strengths made us swell with pride and gave us more fuel to achieve our goals.

Recognition for hard work, valuable skills, helpful advice, or good values can be hugely motivating if it feels genuine and specific. Furthermore, people are more likely to succeed when using their strengths—a message explored in depth by Marcus Buckingham and Donald Clifton in *Now, Discover Your Strengths* and Tom Rath in *StrengthsFinder 2.0*.

For example, if someone on your team loves ramping up new hires and is good at it, find opportunities for her to do more in that vein—maybe mentor an intern or become an informal coach to others. If you have a community builder who is already naturally organizing team lunches, ask him if he'd be interested in running certain meetings.

In each case, you're giving someone an opportunity to grow in a way that speaks to their interests and strengths. "There is one quality that sets truly great managers apart from the rest: they discover what is unique about each person and then capitalize on it," says Buckingham, the renowned management consultant who has studied hundreds of organizations and leaders. "The job of a manager . . . is to turn one person's particular talent into performance."

If you take this principle of managing to strengths one step further, you'll find that it also applies to teams.

If you have five people on your team, four of whom are doing well and one who isn't, you may feel like you should focus most of your time and energy on the struggling report because you want to "fix" the problem. But in the same way that individuals should play to their strengths, so should you pay attention to your team's top talent—the people who are doing well and could be doing even better. Don't let the worst performers dominate your time—try to diagnose, address, and resolve their issues as swiftly as you can.

This is counterintuitive because your strongest reports aren't likely asking for your help. Going back to the lemonade stand example from Chapter One, if Toby is selling thirty cups of lemonade an hour and Henry is selling only ten cups, you might feel compelled to spend a majority of your time with Henry to improve his output. But if coaching Toby gets him to even a 10 percent improvement, he'll be selling an extra three cups. You'd have to help Henry do 33 percent better to get the same result, which will probably be much harder to achieve.

Good CEOs know that they should double down on the projects that are working and put more people, resources, and attention on those rather than get every single project to the point of "not failing." Similarly, good investors know that helping to identify and grow a single start-up into the next billion-dollar company is worth dozens of other investments that lose money. The rising stars on your team may not be clamoring for your attention, but if you help them to dream bigger and become more capable leaders, you'll be amazed at how much more your team can do as a whole.

THE ONE THING YOU SHOULDN'T TOLERATE ON YOUR TEAM

There is a certain archetype of the brilliant lone wolf who, though he regularly puts others down, manages to come out the hero because he is simply heads and tails more capable than anyone else. It's a romantic notion in popular media—Sherlock Holmes, Miranda Priestly, Tony Stark—but in real life, these people are not who you want on your team no matter how talented they are. Instead of a multiplier effect, you get a divider effect: the presence of this person makes the rest of your team less effective.

Stanford professor Robert I. Sutton described this phenomenon in his now famous book *The No Asshole Rule*. He defines an asshole as someone who makes other people feel worse about themselves or who specifically targets people less powerful than him or her.

I once worked with a particular individual who was creative and prolific but who was so wrapped up in his own opinions that if you disagreed with him and you were less senior, he'd dismiss you as being terrible at your job. While he could have been a source of inspiration to others, his teammates went out of their way to avoid him because, as one person put it to me bluntly, "He makes you feel like an idiot." A huge amount of time was spent dealing with the frayed relationships in his wake.

With the benefit of hindsight, it's easy to recognize the aura of toxicity that this person created. But as an inexperienced manager, I didn't always see it clearly. *He does a lot of impressive work*, I thought to myself.

What I later realized is that the team actually becomes *better off* when brilliant assholes leave. Yes, you lose out on their individual contributions, but the fog lifts for everyone else. They can let their guard down. Collaboration becomes more honest and productive, so the work of the team as a whole improves.

The second thing I learned is that it is possible to find people who are just as talented *and* who are humble and kind. It's not an either-or, as the movies would have you believe. You can and should hold the bar high for collaboration. These people are out there. Don't compromise your values for someone who thinks it's okay to bully others. You and your team deserve better.

The third lesson is that assholes can change if the culture you set is clear that it won't tolerate them. You'll learn more about establishing a healthy team culture in Chapter Ten.

YOU DON'T ALWAYS HAVE TO MAKE IT WORK

When I first started managing, I made the mistake of thinking my job was to always "make it work." I reasoned that if two smart, well-intentioned individuals couldn't agree, then surely it must be the result of some misunderstanding. My job, therefore, was to shed clarity on the matter and get everyone to shake hands and sing campfire songs together again.

When one of my reports would bring up a complaint about someone else, say, a coworker who never seemed to listen to his suggestions, I'd try to help him see the other side—*maybe she doesn't know you feel this way. Maybe you're missing context. Have you tried talking to her?*

I'd then seek out the other party and do the same: explain the issue, understand her perspective, and encourage a get-together to negotiate peace. The entire time, I'd be thinking, *Of course there is a productive way out of this.*

I didn't always succeed. Once, another manager came to me and explained that he couldn't work productively with one of my reports. I pushed back, sure that whatever they disagreed about could be resolved. I spent my next week going back and forth between the two of them. After my fourth meeting with the other manager, he said to me in exasperation, "You're trying to save a situation that isn't worth your time, my time, or your report's time to save." He was right. The two of them had very different values and working styles, and they'd both be happier if they weren't on the same project.

Over the years, I've also had some wonderful team members leave because they were looking for something different. At first, it was hard not to take each departure as a personal failure. I couldn't reconcile how someone I liked so much could not work out with a team I cared so much about. It felt like LEGO pieces not fitting together, like peas and carrots refusing to cooperate. Surely I had done something wrong!

But, slowly, my perspective changed. I now understand that personal and organizational values play a huge role in whether someone will be happy on a given team.

Call it what you want—fit, motivation, chemistry—but the things a person cares about must also be what the team (and company) cares about.

If not, then that person might find themselves in frequent misalignment with what they want for their own career.

If the fit just isn't right on a particular team, sometimes a move within the same organization solves the issue—a new environment plus a different problem to noodle on is often exactly what's needed. If that doesn't work, then perhaps the fit is with the company as a whole, in which case parting ways may be the best outcome for everyone.

Dating is a good analogy. You can imagine a person who is a catch by all accounts—kind, responsible, interesting, in possession of a winning smile—but with whom you'd struggle to be in a relationship. Maybe they're a champion skydiver and you have a fear of heights. Maybe they want a van full of kids and you don't see that in your future. Maybe they're seeking to grow roots but your eyes are still dreamy with wanderlust. That's fine. They just weren't right for you.

These days, I spend a lot of time trying to understand what potential candidates value, as well as being transparent about what my company and I value. If my descriptions have them nodding along like it's music to their ears, then they're going to love this job. If not, that's okay too. Even if they have the exact skills that I'm looking for, it's better not to try to fit a round peg into a square hole. Each of us ought to be working in an environment that we love with the people who share our passions. And if along the way we realize that we're meant to do something else, let's celebrate that instead of seeing it as a failure.

MAKE PEOPLE MOVES QUICKLY

When I first started managing, I considered my role above all to be a champion for my team. It was my job to support them, defend them, and listen to them. If a report was struggling to do quality work, not being productive, or decreasing team morale, I'd think to myself, *If I don't step up and show some empathy, who else will?*

Nobody. As their manager, this was my job. And everyone deserves a second chance.

Unfortunately, 80 percent of the time, that effort—extra 1:1s, help on projects, conversations with peers, pep talks—ultimately proved futile.

We've already discussed the main reasons why someone might not be doing great work: they aren't aware of what "great" looks like, their aspirations aren't a fit with what the role needs, they don't feel appreciated, they lack the skills, or they bring others down.

Issues of awareness or lack of appreciation can usually be addressed with a series of honest conversations. But if what motivates a person simply doesn't jibe with the values of the team, then a bunch of pep talks may relieve short-term symptoms, but they don't provide a cure.

For example, one of my reports—we'll call him Fred—was passionate about designing for cutting-edge technologies. His work would often incorporate inventive new interactions that were a delight to experience on state-of-the-art phones.

But our team designs products used by billions of people all over the world, and the vast majority do not have the latest technology. They may be on phones with poor network connections or low storage space. Because of this, our team prioritizes work that is valuable to the greatest number of people, which means designing within many constraints. This mismatch of values meant that Fred grew frustrated whenever his bold, blue-sky concepts were rejected in favor of ideas that were more practical.

Similarly, if your report has a fundamental skills gap that is affecting her ability to do the job well, it's unreasonable to expect that even the best coaching will turn things around within a few months. A report of mine whom we'll call Sarah had a knack for putting out thoughtful designs but struggled to stay organized. She operated best in highly structured environments that offered strong project management support; however, at our organization, we take a bottom-up approach where all employees are expected to manage their own time effectively. In that context, Sarah would often miss deadlines or forget about assignments she'd agreed to take on.

As a new manager, I'd pour a ton of energy—sometimes even 50 percent of my week—into the Freds and Sarahs of the team. I'd have long conversations with them, work together to make changes, hope that things would get better, and then see the same patterns resurface. It was incredibly draining. But I thought this was how it had to be for me to show my care as a manager.

The turning point was when I realized that this cycle wasn't just hard for me, it was even worse for my report. The person I was trying to help would feel stressed out because he knew he wasn't doing well, and my "help" felt like the Eye of Sauron watching his every move. Meanwhile, the rest of my team would wait impatiently for things to get better because they also felt the effects of a struggling teammate.

At the end of the day, if you don't believe someone is set up to succeed in his current role, the kindest thing you can do is to be honest with him and support him in moving on. Former General Electric CEO Jack Welch argues that protecting low performers only increases the damage when, inevitably, a manager is forced to let them go. "What I think is brutal and 'false kindness' is keeping people around who aren't going to grow and prosper. There's no cruelty like waiting and telling people late in their careers that they don't belong."

You have two options at this point: help someone find a new role in your organization or let him or her go.

The first option should always be considered because if there is a better role out there that's more aligned with your report's interests and skills, then that's a great outcome for both the person and your company. Remember Fred, who loved working on innovative new designs? He ended up joining another team specifically focused on emerging technologies, and he thrived in his new role.

Tread carefully, though. Because the idea of firing someone feels so unpleasant, managers may hesitate to let a report go even when it's the best thing for that person or the organization. Avoid shuffling around people who lack the right skills or who exhibit toxic behavior.

A good question to ask is: *If this person were not already at the organization, would I recommend that another team hire him or her knowing what I know?* Sarah, the employee who struggled with operating independently, was not somebody who I could see being successful anywhere within the company.

When you decide to let someone go, do it respectfully and directly. Don't open it up to discussion (it isn't one), and don't regard it as a failure on the part of your report. (As Netflix's former chief talent officer, Patty McCord, reflects, "Why do we call it 'getting fired'? Are we shooting people?")

Just because your report didn't work out on your team doesn't mean it's on him—in fact, I'm often reminded of the wise words of my friend Robyn Morris: "Perhaps it's *you* who shouldn't be his manager, not the other way around." Perhaps you made the call to hire him when his skills weren't what the team needed. Or perhaps you put him on projects that weren't a good match. Caring about people means owning that your relationship is a two-way street.

Firing someone can be emotional and challenging not just for the person being fired but also for you and the team. Be compassionate in examining the past, but focus on the future and don't prolong the breakup. Help your report get on the best possible path toward the next chapter, and use the experience to become a better manager.

The good news is that letting people go is an extreme situation. More commonly, the right coaching can help your reports understand what to aspire to, how to overcome the habits that are holding them back, and how to grow their impact.

Great managers are excellent coaches, and the secret sauce to coaching is the topic of our next chapter—giving effective feedback.

Chapter Four

The Art of Feedback

AVOID

ASPIRE

The worst feedback I ever got came in an email from a former intern, Drew Hamlin. He regularly wrote to our design team during the school year with his observations about our work. In one message, he pointed out a particular misalignment of elements on the screen, writing, "Did you mean to make this so terrible?"

We knew he asked this in earnestness, not malice, but it was definitely lesson one in how *not* to give feedback. Fortunately, we didn't read too much into his words. Impressed by his passion and proactivity, we hired him after he graduated. A few years later, he became a beloved manager. In a funny twist of fate, Drew was one of the primary architects of our current critique practice. To this day, we continue to poke fun at him for lobbing "the world's worst critique."

The best feedback I ever got came from my former report Robyn. Once, when I asked him what I could be doing better, he took a deep breath and said, "Julie, sometimes I get the feeling that when I'm doing well, you're on my side and the two of us are great. But when I'm not doing as well, our relationship suffers, and I don't feel that you trust me as much." He proceeded to share a few examples of things I had said that made him feel this way, delivered with kindness and honesty. This single piece of feedback transformed my entire perspective on management.

Unfortunately, most people struggle with giving feedback. Sometimes, we don't feel like we have anything useful to say. Or if we do have a critical thought, we stay silent because we worry about hurting others' feelings. When something isn't broken, we accept that it's good enough, so why say more? And when we do give feedback, we put ourselves at risk because it might be perceived as "too vague to be helpful" or "too emotionally charged to be effective." Given all this, it's no wonder that new managers often find this the most challenging part of the job.

For a leader, giving feedback—both when things are going well and when they aren't—is one of the most fundamental aspects of the job. Mastering this skill means that you can knock down two of the biggest barriers preventing your reports from doing great work—unclear expectations and inadequate skills—so that they know exactly where to aim and how to hit the target.

WHAT DOES GREAT FEEDBACK LOOK LIKE?

Think of the best feedback you've ever received. Why was it so meaningful to you?

I'm willing to bet that the reason you remember it is because *the feedback inspired you to change your behavior, which resulted in your life getting better.*

Feedback, at its best, transforms people in ways they're proud of. There's no question that I'm a better manager today because of that eye-opening conversation with Robyn.

So what constitutes "feedback"? Early in my career, I defined it as "suggestions for improvement." The canonical example in my head was design critique. I figured that giving feedback meant identifying a problem and coming up with some possible solutions.

That turned out to be quite a narrow definition. There's a whole swath of things beyond "suggestions for improvement" that can inspire someone to take positive action. For one, feedback doesn't have to be critical. Praise is often more motivating than criticism. And for another, you don't always have to start with a problem.

Below, you'll find the four most common ways to inspire a change in behavior.

Set Clear Expectations at the Beginning

Imagine that you decide to hire a trainer to improve your workouts. Does she immediately ask you to do some push-ups before giving you any pointers?

No. The first thing she'll do after introductions is sit down with you to discuss your goals. Then, she'll tell you what you should expect from training and how you can make the most of it. Though her advice won't yet be specifically tailored to you, it's what she thinks you need to know given her experience training others.

It may seem counterintuitive, but the feedback process should begin before any work does. At that point, you should agree on what success looks like—whether for a given project or for a given time period—get ahead of any expected issues, and lay the foundation for productive feedback sessions in the future. It's like starting a journey with a well-marked map versus blindly walking a few miles and then asking if you're on track.

During this phase, make sure you address the following:

- What a great job looks like for your report, compared to a mediocre or bad job
- What advice you have to help your report get started on the right foot
- Common pitfalls your report should avoid

> In your first three months on the job, I expect that you'll build good relationships with your team, be able to ramp up on a small-scale "starter" project, and then share your first design iteration for review. I don't expect that you'll get the green light on it right away, but if you do, that would be knocking it out of the park.

Here's what success looks like for the next meeting you run: the different options are framed clearly, everyone feels like their point of view is well represented, and a decision is made.

Give Task-Specific Feedback as Frequently as You Can

As the name "task-specific" implies, you provide this kind of feedback about something that someone did after the fact. For example, after your report presents an analysis, tell her what you thought she did well and what could go better in the future. Be as precise and as detailed as you can.

This is the easiest type of feedback to give because it's focused on the *what* rather than the *who*, so it feels less personal. If you find yourself struggling to get into the habit of giving feedback, start with this category.

Task-specific feedback is most effective when the action performed is still fresh in your report's memory, so share it as soon as you can. Unless the task is significant, like a high-stakes presentation, dropping a note via email or chat within the day can work just as well as giving the feedback face-to-face.

At its best, task-specific feedback becomes a lightweight, habitual part of your day, and your reports benefit from getting small doses of coaching in everything you see them do.

That research report you shared yesterday was excellent. The way you succinctly summarized the most important findings at the top made it easy to process. The particular insight about X was really useful.

Quick note about the presentation you gave this morning: I noticed you went straight to the proposal without explaining how you got there. This made it hard to assess why it was the best

path. Next time, try spending a few minutes walking through
your process and what alternatives you considered.

Share Behavioral Feedback Thoughtfully and Regularly

When you zoom out and look at many examples of task-specific feedback for a report, what themes emerge? Does he make decisions quickly or slowly? Is he a process wizard or an unconventional thinker? Does he gravitate toward pragmatic or idealistic solutions?

Asking this question about themes helps you reflect on your report's unique strengths or areas of development as shown in his patterns of behavior.

Behavioral feedback is useful because it provides a level of personalization and depth that is missing from task-specific feedback. By connecting the dots across multiple examples, you can help people understand how their unique interests, personalities, and habits affect their ability to have impact.

When you give behavioral feedback, you are making a statement about how you perceive that person, so your words need to be thoughtfully considered and supported with specific examples to explain why you feel that way. It's best discussed in person so the receiver can ask questions and engage in a back-and-forth with you.

Behavioral feedback helps people understand the reality of how others see them, which may be different than how they see themselves. It can feel difficult to talk about because it *is* so personal—a friend of mine likens it to "therapy sessions"—but at its best, you help your reports walk away with a deeper understanding of themselves and how they can be more effective.

When people ask you questions about your work, your tone is
often defensive. For example, when Sally left a comment on

your code, you replied with "just trust me." This disregarded the substance of her feedback and made you appear less trustworthy.

Your recruiting skills are top-notch. Candidates often say they leave a conversation with you feeling more inspired than when they began. You also have a keen sense for suggesting the right people for the right roles. For example, you identified John for Project X a year ago, and now he's thriving.

Collect 360-Degree Feedback for Maximum Objectivity

Three-hundred-and-sixty-degree feedback is feedback aggregated from multiple perspectives, which means it tends to be a more complete and objective view of how someone is doing. For example, if your report led a brainstorming session, instead of sending just *your* task-specific feedback, you might collect and share what the rest of the room thought as well. Or if it's time for your report's annual performance review, instead of relying on just your own observations, getting behavioral feedback from the handful of colleagues she works closest with will result in better insights.

Many companies run a 360-feedback process once or twice a year. If it's not formally done, you can gather the feedback yourself. Every quarter, for each report, I send a short email to a handful of his or her closest collaborators asking: a) What is X doing especially well that X should do more of?, and b) What should X change or stop doing?

The thoroughness of 360-degree feedback means that it takes more time to gather, so it's not practical to do more than a handful of times a year. However, it's particularly useful when you lack deep context on your report's day-to-day. Because it's so comprehensive, you should set up a meeting with your report to discuss

the feedback in person, as well as document the learnings in writing so that both of you can refer to it in the future.

> *Your peers give you a lot of props for how you managed the bud-
> get crisis. This was important and difficult work, and your calm
> demeanor, excellent listening skills, and rational arguments
> helped the team get to a good outcome.*

> *One of the consistent themes from your 360-feedback is that
> your plans need more rigor. An example is how you left out the
> edge case of senior discounts in your pricing proposal, which re-
> sulted in incorrect projections. This pattern of small errors
> across your work is starting to undermine your credibility.*

EVERY MAJOR DISAPPOINTMENT IS A FAILURE TO SET EXPECTATIONS

Many years ago, my former manager Kate Aronowitz casually
asked me how my team was doing. "Everyone's doing well," I replied, "with one exception" (we'll call him Albert). "Oh?" she said,
cocking her head. "What's going on with Albert?"

I sighed and launched into my concerns: The first version of his
recent work had wildly missed the mark, and even after three
rounds of feedback, it wasn't quite there. His engineers were getting impatient, and the other designers wondered why he consistently ignored their suggestions.

"So is he meeting expectations?" Kate asked. I paused, thought
about it for a second, and then said no. She raised an eyebrow.
"And have you told him that *explicitly*?"

"Well . . ." I trailed off. I had given Albert plenty of task-specific
feedback, but I wasn't direct about how his performance was

trending. We were six weeks away from doing a company-wide 360-feedback cycle, and I assumed we would talk about it then. I could tell from Kate's expression that I was in for a learning moment.

"If the first time he hears that he's not meeting expectations is during his performance review, it's going to feel terrible," she said. She went on to explain that because our reviews are meant to summarize performance from the past six months, if Albert was indeed not meeting expectations for most of that time, I should have told him that much earlier.

She was right. If Albert were to get a rude shock next month, he'd have three possible explanations for what happened, none of which are good.

1. *The review isn't fair. If things really were so dire, why hasn't this come up until now? This must be a mistake.*

2. *The review is fair, but my manager was negligent and didn't realize I was underperforming until the end of the half.*

3. *The review is fair, but my manager wasn't honest in sharing feedback with me along the way, so I didn't have a chance to improve.*

I was at risk of falling into bucket three. Luckily, I still had time to put the lesson into action. The sooner that Albert internalized he was not meeting expectations, the quicker he could potentially turn things around, and the smoother our future performance conversations would go.

Nobody likes being taken by surprise with bad news. Following are some examples of how setting expectations early can preempt future disappointments.

Your Report Has Made It Clear That She Wants a Promotion

You don't think it's likely to happen within the next six months. If you wait until the next performance review to tell her, she'll have spent months wondering if she got the promotion and then be disappointed.

Instead, if you say right away, "I understand that you'd like to work toward a promotion, but here are the gaps I'm seeing . . . ," you're showing that you want to help her reach her goal. Spell out what your promotion criteria are. Over the next few months, coach her and give her frequent feedback on how she's doing relative to those expectations. That way, she'll never have to wonder.

You've Just Assigned a Challenging New Project to Your Report

Because this project is high stakes, you'd like to keep a close eye on how it's going. If you frequently drop in and ask for an update or give unsolicited feedback, you risk making your report feel disempowered. He'll be constantly checking over his shoulder, paranoid that you're just around the corner.

At the same time, you don't want to wait a month before reviewing the work. If it's not heading down the right track, you'd like to know sooner rather than later.

Here, setting expectations helps with both problems. At the beginning of the project, let your report know how you're planning to be involved. Be explicit that you'd like to review the work twice a week and talk through the most important problems together. Tell him which decisions you expect to make, and which he should make.

Managers who pop in out of the blue and throw down new requirements can breed resentment with their team (just Google the term "Swoop and Poop.") But managers who proactively lay out what they care about and how they want to engage in projects rarely encounter those tensions.

Your Team Has Set a Goal to Launch in October

Let's say your team learns in June that they're unlikely to be ready in October. Would you prefer for them to tell you shortly before launch or right away?

I don't know any manager who would choose to know later. At that point, a lot more work will be wasted—money spent on marketing, press plans that need to be redone, sales forecasts that are no longer accurate. Plus, you're going to wonder why your team didn't tell you sooner—was it incompetence or was it deceit?

If you're informed in June, then you have more options. You could decide to put more people on the project or cut features to hit your October goal. Or you could accept the delay and point everyone toward a new launch date.

And yet, your team may resist telling you directly, "We don't think we can make the October goal." They might believe they can still turn things around. Or they might fear getting into trouble. By setting expectations that you'd like to hear about any concerns with the launch date as soon as possible, you establish that it's safe to talk about problems even in the early phases.

It's impossible to expect perfection. We are only human. Failures will occur, projects will miss deadlines, and people will make mistakes. That's okay. But when these things happen, readjusting expectations as quickly as possible helps people recover from errors with grace. You demonstrate care and maturity when you preempt bigger issues down the road.

Whenever you find yourself deeply disappointed, or disappointing someone else, ask yourself: Where did I miss out on setting clear expectations, and how might I do better in the future?

YOUR FEEDBACK ONLY COUNTS IF IT MAKES THINGS BETTER

One of my reports—we'll call him George—had a tendency to be long-winded when he spoke. During presentations, the audience would lose the thread of his point and he'd be met with a room of blank faces. If I asked for a quick two-line update, he'd give me a five-minute explanation. I saw that this made people less likely to listen to him, so one day, I sat him down and told him. George took it well, and after the conversation, I gave myself a hearty pat on the back. Go, me! I'd given helpful feedback and done my duty as a manager.

A few weeks later, when George led another presentation, the exact same thing happened: His remarks went into details beyond what the audience could comprehend in thirty minutes. I was baffled. Hadn't we just talked about this?

In our next conversation, I asked him why he didn't work on simplifying his presentation. He frowned. "But I *did* work on it," he insisted. He showed me how he had included a table of contents and changed the order in which he talked about things.

That was when I realized it was *I* who misunderstood: George *had* heard the feedback. The issue was that he didn't see what was complicated about the way he explained things. And if he couldn't see it, he couldn't fix it.

I might feel accomplished in pointing out the problem, but that's not the point if it doesn't actually help him. The mark of a great coach is that others improve under your guidance. Maybe you'd like to see your reports dream bigger, accomplish more, or overcome the barriers that get in their way. The question that should always be in the back of your mind is: Does my feedback lead to the change I'm hoping for?

Broken down one level further, consider how you're doing with each of the following.

Am I Giving Feedback Often Enough?

I've read thousands of reviews written by reports about their managers, and the most common response to the question "How could your manager better support you?" is simply "Give me more feedback."

It's worth pausing for a moment: before getting deep into the nitty-gritty of the *how*, the first step is simply to *give feedback more often* and remind yourself that you're probably not doing it enough.

Every time you see one of your reports in action—delivering a project, interacting with a customer, negotiating a sale, speaking up in a meeting—see if there's something useful you can tell her. Strive for at least 50 percent positive feedback so she knows what she's doing well—"You made a particularly keen observation" or "You showed a lot of empathy in that interaction." If you hear something positive from a colleague, pass it along. Or, if you have a suggestion for improvement, even if it's small, tell her that as well—"You said a lot in that meeting, which made it hard for others to get in a word."

At the same time, watch out for only ever giving task-specific feedback. The second most common ask from reports is: "Give me more feedback related to my skills and my career trajectory." I knew a manager who was a designer's designer and a top-notch creative director. He could casually glance at a mock-up and tell you if the spacing between the icons was two pixels off. His team always knew where he stood on their work. However, in their upward reviews, I would read comments like, "I want to understand my manager's opinion on how I'm progressing" or "I want to have conversations about my career goals and how to achieve them." His team longed for additional attention about *them* as people, not just on their output.

If you find that your frequency of feedback is low, one tactic

I've found helpful is to devote a single 1:1 every month to *just* discussing behavioral feedback and career goals.

Is My Feedback Being Heard?

I once had a report—we'll call her Amy—who I didn't feel was operating at her full potential. While others on the team set ambitious goals and worked hard to hit them, she shied away from challenging projects and completed the ones she had slowly. She took long lunches and often did unrelated personal tasks at her desk. I realized I needed to have a serious conversation with her about her low output.

I spent a week preparing. I wrote down all my talking points, ran them by a colleague for advice, and rehearsed the conversation in front of a mirror. When the time came, I walked in and delivered the feedback clearly. I walked out feeling like a huge weight had been lifted from my shoulders.

A few days later, another colleague approached me and asked if we could chat in private about Amy. When we were alone, she said, "I'm sure you didn't mean it this way, but you should know that Amy thinks you're overstepping and micromanaging her time. Why did you say that she shouldn't be allowed to have lunch or browse the internet at work?"

Hearing this, I was shocked. In my talk with Amy, I had briefly mentioned the long lunches and non-work activity as two data points among others that made me wonder about her motivation. But the point I really wanted to make was about her low productivity. If she was a top performer, this issue would never have come up. Conversely, if she worked double the hours of everyone else but didn't accomplish much, I'd still be concerned.

If you've ever played a game of telephone as a kid, you know this to be true: What you intend to say and what the listener hears are not always the same. You might think you're being clear when in fact you're saying too much, or too little, or sending a different message through your body language. (I've been told, for example, that I'm prone to rambling, which can make it hard to understand my main point, and that my friendliness can mask the seriousness of a tough message.) Add to that the listener's confirmation bias—our tendency to recall things that confirm preexisting beliefs—and it's no wonder that messages get muddled in translation.

Ed Batista, an executive coach and instructor at Stanford Graduate School of Business, explains that part of the reason feedback doesn't stick is that the recipient often views the conversation as a threat, so his adrenaline-fueled fight-or-flight instinct kicks in. When feedback is given, Batista writes, the listener's "heart rate and blood pressure are almost certain to increase, [accompanied by] a cascade of neurological and physiological events that impair the ability to process complex information and react thoughtfully. When people are in the grip of a threat response, they're less capable of absorbing and applying your observations."

The best way to make your feedback heard is to make the listener feel safe, and to show that you're saying it because you care about her and want her to succeed. If you come off with even a whiff of an ulterior motive—you want to be right, you're judging her, you're annoyed or impatient—the message won't get through.

This is why positive feedback is so effective. Just ask any preschool teacher or pet owner, and they'll tell you that recognizing what's going well is more likely to change behavior than only pointing out mistakes. Saying, "Hey, I thought that thing you did was awesome," reinforces what you'd like to see more of without being threatening.

When you do have critical feedback to share, approach it with a sense of curiosity and an honest desire to understand your report's perspective. One simple way to do this is to state your point directly and then follow up with, "Does this feedback resonate with you? Why or why not?" Most of the time when I ask this question, the answer is yes, and now the person has both acknowledged and reflected on the feedback, so it's more likely to stick. If the answer is no, that's fine as well—now we can discuss why that is, and what would make the feedback more useful.

At the end of a conversation, when you're not sure whether you've been heard, there are a few things you can do. The first is a verbal confirmation: "Okay, let's make sure we're on the same page—what are your takeaways and next steps?" The second is to summarize via email what was discussed. Writing can clarify the points being made as well as be reread and referenced in the future.

The third tactic is to help the person hear the same message many times and from many sources. For example, try dedicating multiple 1:1s to talking about particularly tough areas of growth with your report. Gather and share 360-degree feedback when you suspect your message isn't landing—it's a powerful way to relay that others are seeing the same thing. One manager I know takes it even further—whenever he gets feedback about one of his reports from someone else, he always asks that person, "Would you be comfortable sharing that feedback directly with X?" He reasons that there will be less of a distortion effect if he removes himself as a middleman and that the feedback will be more clearly heard and internalized.

Does My Feedback Lead to Positive Action?

When I asked George to simplify his communication, the problem wasn't that he didn't hear the message. He did—he just didn't know what to do with it. As a result, my feedback wasn't helpful.

How do you ensure that your feedback can be acted upon? Remember these three tips.

1. Make your feedback as specific as possible. When I told George, "Your presentation was complicated and people had a hard time understanding it," I was assuming that his definition of *complicated* and mine were the same. This is rarely the case, so my feedback ended up sounding vague. Which aspects were complicated? What was said, exactly, that led to people being confused?

Use clear examples that get at the *why* so it's easier for the recipient to know what you mean.

> *You lost the room when you shared seven goals for the review instead of just one or two. It's hard to remember them all, so the priorities felt unclear.*

> *At the end, you showed three different directions for where we could go from here, but you didn't give us your recommendations or how to think about the pros and cons of each option. As a result, people were confused about the next steps.*

2. Clarify what success looks and feels like. Even if your feedback is specific, heard, and understood, it can still be hard for the other person to have a clear picture of what they should aspire to. Some years ago, at a design review, my manager Chris told us that our proposed designs showing a registration form felt too "heavy."

One of the designers in the room suggested that we change the outline stroke of the form field boxes from blue to gray and that we put a little more space between them. "It'll feel lighter and more breathable," he said. Chris thought about it. "Think of the lines at Disneyland," he finally said. "You're actually waiting in a really long line, but because you're going from one small room to another, it doesn't feel like the line is overwhelming. That's what I'm going for." Instantly, we had a clear sense of how to improve the flow—break the one long form into a series of smaller ones.

3. Suggest next steps. Often the easiest way to help your report translate your feedback into action is to share what you think the next steps should be. Be clear about whether you're setting an expectation or merely offering a suggestion. Also, beware of overdoing this—if you're always dictating what should happen next, you're not empowering your team to learn to solve problems on their own. A softer approach is to ask your report, "So what do you think the next steps should be?" and let them guide the discussion.

> *Can you do another pass on this report with the changes we discussed today, and I'll set up the next review for Thursday?*

> *One suggestion that might help you with your next presentation is using the rule of threes—no more than three goals, three sections, and three bullets per slide.*

> *Given what we just talked about, what are your next steps?*

DELIVERING CRITICAL FEEDBACK OR BAD NEWS

Telling your report something disappointing is both important and unavoidable. Here, the *how* matters tremendously. You can convey the same point a dozen different ways—by varying your chosen words, your tone, or your body language. Observe:

1. *You're such a screwup. What am I going to do with you?*

2. *Your work is terrible, and I need to know how you're going to fix it.*

3. *I'm concerned about the quality of work that I've been seeing from you recently. Can we talk about that?*

4. *Your last few deliverables weren't comprehensive enough to hit the mark, so let's discuss why that is and how to address it.*

5. *I have a few questions about your latest work—do you have a moment to walk me through it?*

Common sense says that number one is to be avoided like the plague. Nothing good comes out of accusing someone of being a screwup. Charged language or declarations that are personal ("you're thoughtless" instead of "your action was thoughtless") immediately puts the other person on the defensive. Suddenly you're a threat they're protecting themselves from, and it's unlikely they're going to sit down and listen to what you have to say after that.

Number two isn't personal, but *terrible* is still a strong word. It feels like a one-way scolding where you're acting as the judge, and the burden of fixing things falls entirely on your report.

Nobody thinking rationally intends to say numbers one or two, but it happens. We get upset or emotional. Someone says something that pisses us off and all of a sudden, we're seeing red and want to give them a piece of our mind. The best advice for prevention? Don't engage when you are upset. We regret the things we say in anger, and while bridges take months or years to build, they can be burned in an instant. So recognize when that vein on your forehead is starting to bulge, take a deep breath, say, "Let's talk about this later," and exit stage left.

Number five (*I have a few questions about your latest work—do you have a moment to walk me through it?*) might seem like an attractive opener (and is how I used to begin many of my critical feedback sessions), but it's the scared manager's choice. You're afraid of upsetting your report or you're not sure if your opinion is 100 percent right, so you phrase your concerns as "questions." While it's healthy to approach giving feedback with a curious mindset—*what's the other side of the story?*—don't lose the plot. At best, framing your worries as questions feels disingenuous, and at worst, your report will miss that you're actually concerned, which means nothing will change.

The best way to give critical feedback is to deliver it directly and dispassionately. Plainly say what you perceive the issue to be, what made you feel that way, and how you'd like to work together to resolve the concern. Both number three (*I'm concerned about the quality of work that I've been seeing from you recently*) and four (*Your last few deliverables weren't comprehensive enough to hit the mark*) accomplish that, although number four gets a slight edge because it's more specific in describing the concern.

If you need a template, try this:

> *When I [heard/observed/reflected on] your [action/behavior/ output], I felt concerned because . . .*

> *I'd like to understand your perspective and talk about how we can resolve this.*

Don't start with a long preamble. Don't try to sugarcoat a tough message or pad it with "softer" points. As a new manager, I read advice that the best way to deliver critical feedback was in a "compliment sandwich," where you start out with a positive observation, then slide in your suggestion for improvement, then close with another pat on the back, as if the only way veggies can be palatable is if they're surrounded by a bunch of marshmallows.

I find this ineffective—lobbing over a few superficial words of praise to temper a hard message comes off as insincere. Plus, the thing you actually want them to pay attention to might be lost. Which of the below do you think is more effective at getting people to put away their phone?

> *Hey, nice job bringing up the point about budgeting in the last meeting. By the way, try not to use your phone so much next*

time, as it can be distracting. But those next steps you took us through were really well framed!

Hey, I noticed that when you use your phone in meetings, it's distracting because it suggests that the meeting isn't worth paying attention to. Can we agree to no phones in the future?

If you are delivering bad news about a decision—you decided to pick someone else for a coveted position, you're pulling your report off the project, you no longer have a role for this person on your team, etc.—the decision should be the first thing out of your mouth when you both sit down.

I've decided to go with somebody else to lead this initiative . . .

Own the decision. Be firm, and don't open it up for discussion. I failed at this many times in the past because I hated being the bearer of bad news. So I'd try to position the decision as something we were making together. "I want to discuss the leadership role on Project Z," I'd say. "I'm concerned that you won't have the time for it. You're already doing so much on X and Y. So I think it'd be good for somebody else to lead Z. What do you think?"

The problem was, if nothing my report said could convince me to change my mind, it's insincere to act as if she had had a say. What if she responds, "Actually, I do have the time for it"? Or if she brings up a slew of other reasons why she's the best candidate? I'd only be scrambling to give her another excuse, which would make her feel unheard.

When you give feedback or make a decision, your report may not agree with it. That's okay. Keep in mind that some decisions are yours to make. You are the person ultimately held accountable for the output of your team, and you may have more information or a different perspective on the right path forward.

Managing through consensus may feel like a good idea because you won't offend anyone, but I can't think of a single influential leader who hasn't had to go out on a limb and do something somebody else disagreed with. Acknowledge the disagreement respectfully, then move on. "I recognize that you may not agree with my decision, but I'm asking for your cooperation in moving forward."

Ultimately, what I've learned about giving feedback—even the most difficult feedback—is that people are not fragile flowers. No report has ever said to me, "Please treat me with kid gloves." Instead, they say: "I want your feedback to help me improve." They tell me, "I'd like you to be honest and direct with me." How many of us don't want the same? Telling it straight is a sign of respect.

"It's brutally hard to tell people when they are screwing up," writes Kim Scott, a former Google manager and the author of *Radical Candor.* "You don't *want* to hurt anyone's feelings; that's because you're not a sadist. You don't want that person or the rest of the team to think you're a jerk. Plus, you've been told since you learned to talk, 'If you don't have anything nice to say, don't say anything at all.' Now all of a sudden it's your *job* to say it. You've got to undo a lifetime of training."

I'm still working on mastering the art of feedback. Every relationship is different, so the frequency, style, and type of feedback that works for one person might not work for someone else. Mistakes are inevitable. But when you give feedback well and you help your report grow as a result, there is no better feeling.

No matter what happens, the skills your team members develop are theirs for life. At Facebook, we have a saying immortalized in posters all over campus: "Feedback is a gift." It costs time and effort to share, but when we have it, we're better off. So let's give it generously.

Chapter Five

Managing Yourself

AVOID

ASPIRE

After I had my first baby, I took three months off from work before returning. I knew the transition back would be hard, but I was not prepared for a "Winter Is Coming" kind of difficult. A few weeks in, I found myself overwhelmed by every little thing. My mind felt like the aftermath of a fourth-grade volcano project, all thick and sticky and slow. When I was at home, I thought about work, and when I was at work, I thought about home. My inability to focus became a source of debilitating stress.

Convinced that I had suddenly transformed into a weepier and less capable person, I asked my manager Chris if I could get an executive coach. That's how I was first introduced to Stacy McCarthy.

The first thing I blurted out to Stacy after we introduced ourselves was that I needed to fix *everything*. In increasingly high-pitched tones, I began listing off one tangled issue after another: areas that were desperately understaffed, people who wanted a change in their roles, a product strategy I didn't agree with, and so on. I imagined her helping me unravel each problem until they were simple, soft balls of yarn ready to be reknit with purpose.

Instead, Stacy listened calmly until I was done. Then she said, "We'll get to all that later, but first, why don't we take a step back? Tell me about you."

I could only blink. Talk about me? But how would that help any one of the seven fires that needed putting out?

But Stacy persisted. She asked me about my past and the road

I'd taken to get here. We talked about the future—the way, *way* future—where she asked me to picture myself at eighty, sitting on a beach and looking back on my life. What did I want to remember? Then she asked me if I would be okay with her interviewing several people who I worked closely with.

I said yes. Two weeks later at our next meeting, she showed up with a twenty-page report *all about me*. There was nothing about the specific problems at hand. Instead, this stack of papers asked deeper questions about how I worked—what were my perceived strengths and weaknesses? In what ways did I impress or annoy those around me? What was my management style like?

I remember the weight of the document as she handed it to me, tucked neatly into a manila folder. I shoved the package in my backpack, unwilling to deal with it. It was only later at night, when the baby was asleep and I was alone with the lights dimmed, that I felt ready to confront the truth. I took a deep breath and turned to the first page.

At that moment, feeling so ungrounded and unsure of myself, I struggled to read the report. I felt like a specimen dissected and laid bare. As much as you try to tell yourself that your inner turmoil lives inside your own head, the truth is that most of us aren't very good actors. People know. They see the faults that you don't want to admit, like how my anxiety was leading to wishy-washy decisions. But they're also kinder to you than you might imagine. I remember tearing up reading comments about how I was kicking ass in ways that I wasn't giving myself credit for.

Looking back, that twenty-page report was one of the best things that happened to my career. It helped me calibrate my own internal compass. It allowed me to understand where my fears were overblown—nobody *actually* thought I was a weepy and less capable person—and where I wasn't paying enough attention— like setting clear expectations for myself and others. Once I knew where I stood, I could start moving forward.

Being a great manager is a highly personal journey, and if you don't have a good handle on yourself, you won't have a good handle on how to best support your team. That's what Stacy was trying to tell me. No matter what obstacles you face, you first need to get deep with knowing *you*—your strengths, your values, your comfort zones, your blind spots, and your biases. When you fully understand yourself, you'll know where your true north lies.

EVERYBODY FEELS LIKE AN IMPOSTER SOMETIMES

I first learned the term *imposter syndrome* during my junior year of college. A professor studying gender differences stood in front of a packed lecture hall, citing example after example that gave me shivers. *Yes! This describes exactly how I feel! I don't deserve to be here in this auditorium, at this dazzling institution, with so many brilliant students. I must have gotten here by error or luck or the grace of the stars. When are they going to figure out that I got good grades because I have a good memory, not because I'm actually smart?*

As a new manager, I've felt this way countless times as well. *Rebekah made a terrible mistake—I have no idea what I'm doing*, my inner voice would whisper every time I fumbled an interaction or struggled to make a decision.

But over the years, I have learned a secret that bears repeating: *Every* manager feels like an imposter sometimes. Every manager was once new, stumbling through interviews and 1:1s and awkward conversations. It's so common that instead of pretending like we are all ducks gliding effortlessly on the surface of the water, we should own up to the furious paddling that is happening beneath.

Imposter syndrome is what makes you feel as though you're the only one with nothing worthwhile to say when you walk into a room full of people you admire. Imposter syndrome is what makes you double-, triple-, or quadruple-check your email before hitting *Send* so that nobody finds any mistakes and figures out you're actually a fraud. Imposter syndrome is the sensation that you're teetering along the edge of a sheer cliff with flailing arms, the whole world watching and waiting to see when you fall.

Here's the thing to remember: feeling this way is totally normal. Linda Hill, a professor at Harvard Business School, has spent years studying the transition into management. "Ask any new manager about the early days of being a boss—indeed, ask any senior executive to recall how he or she felt as a new manager. If you get an honest answer, you'll hear a tale of disorientation and, for some, overwhelming confusion. The new role didn't feel anything like it was supposed to. It felt too big for any one person to handle."

Why does imposter syndrome hit managers so hard? There are two reasons. The first is that you're often looked to for answers. I've had reports tell me about difficult personal issues and ask for my advice. I've gotten requests for permission to do things that the company has never done before, like spend hundreds of thousands of dollars on a new initiative. I've received emotional inquiries from people about countless decisions that I didn't make myself but that I still had to explain.

When the sailing gets rocky, the manager is often the first person others turn to, so it's common to feel an intense pressure to know what to do or say. When you don't, you naturally think: *Am I cut out for this job?*

The second reason is that you are constantly put in the position of doing things you haven't done before. For example, say you have to fire someone. How do you prepare yourself for such a task? It's not like improving your skills in drawing or writing, where you can invest time on nights and weekends to sketch or compose short stories. You can't just snap your fingers and say,

"I'm going to practice firing a lot of people this month." You must actually *go through the real thing* in order to gain the experience you need.

Management isn't an innate skill. There is no such thing as an "all-around great manager" who can transition effortlessly between different leadership roles. We must look at the specific context.

For example, I consider myself a seasoned manager, but if I were to lead a team that was triple the size or in a discipline I don't know well, like sales, I'd probably fail to produce strong results immediately. I'd need to identify my growth areas in that environment—such as how to communicate effectively with a much larger group of people or how to set good sales goals—and spend time honing those skills.

No matter how often imposter syndrome rears its ugly head, it doesn't have to derail you. In these next sections, we'll look at techniques for how to deal with the inevitable doubts and discomfort that will arise.

GET TO BRUTAL HONESTY WITH YOURSELF

Let me tell you a few facts about me: I'm more comfortable in small groups than big ones. I care deeply about understanding first principles. I am more articulate in writing than in person. I need time alone to reflect and process new facts before forming an opinion. I skew toward long-term thinking, which means that I sometimes make impractical short-term decisions. And at the end of the day, nothing gives me more satisfaction than learning and growing.

Why does any of this matter? Because these strengths and weaknesses directly affect how I manage.

Some of my colleagues have completely different superpowers. Among the people I work closest with, one has an ability to take incredibly complex topics and transform them into easy-to-remember frameworks that get at the heart of what really matters. One's strategic prowess is so strong that I'm convinced he must have been a five-star general in a past life. And one amazes me with the way she manages to keep twenty threads moving full steam ahead at the same time. Yet these same folks have told me there are things I do that they admire as well.

The facets of our personality are like the ingredients that come together for a recipe. Could you make a tasty dinner if you peered into your fridge and saw some broccoli, eggs, and chicken? Sure. What if you had potatoes, beef, and spinach? Of course. The key is to understand what works best with what you have.

The world's top leaders come from vastly different molds—some are extroverts (Winston Churchill) and some are introverts (Abraham Lincoln); some are demanding (Margaret Thatcher) and others remind you of a favorite relative (Mother Teresa); some leave a room breathless with their vision (Nelson Mandela) and others prefer to avoid the spotlight (Bill Gates).

The first part in understanding how you lead is to know your strengths—the things you're talented at and love to do. This is crucial because great management typically comes from playing to your strengths rather than from fixing your weaknesses. There are some useful frameworks for understanding your strengths, like *StrengthsFinder 2.0* by Tom Rath or *StandOut* by Marcus Buckingham. If you want to do a quick version, jot down the first thing that comes to mind when you ask yourself the following questions:

- How would the people who know and like me best (family, significant other, close friends) describe me in three words?
  MY ANSWER: *thoughtful, enthusiastic, driven*

- What three qualities do I possess that I am the proudest of?
  MY ANSWER: *curious, reflective, optimistic*

- When I look back on something I did that was successful, what personal traits do I give credit to?
  MY ANSWER: *vision, determination, humility*

- What are the top three most common pieces of positive feedback that I've received from my manager or peers?
  MY ANSWER: *principled, fast learner, long-term thinker*

Like mine, your responses will likely cluster around a few themes. Here, you can see that my strengths are dreaming big, learning quickly, and remaining upbeat. Whatever yours are, remember them and hold them dear. You'll be relying on them time and time again.

The second part of getting to an honest reckoning with yourself is knowing your weaknesses and triggers. Right beneath your list of strengths, answer the following:

- Whenever my worst inner critic sits on my shoulder, what does she yell at me for?
  MY ANSWER: *getting distracted, worrying too much about what others think, not voicing what I believe*

- If a magical fairy were to come and bestow on me three gifts I don't yet have, what would they be?
  MY ANSWER: *bottomless well of confidence, clarity of thought, incredible persuasion*

- What are three things that trigger me? (A trigger is a situation that gets me more worked up than it should.)
  MY ANSWER: *sense of injustice, the idea that someone else thinks I'm incompetent, people with inflated egos*

- What are the top three most common pieces of feedback from my manager or peers on how I could be more effective?

MY ANSWER: *be more direct, take more risks, explain things simply*

Again, you may see some themes emerging. The biggest barriers that get in my way are self-doubt, a tendency to complexify, and not being clear and direct enough.

Okay, now that we've got our lists, the next part is *calibration*, which is making sure that the view we have of ourselves matches reality. This is harder than it sounds. Our self-perception is like a roller coaster. Some days, we struggle with self-compassion. We make a mistake and our inner critic chirps loudly about how we're worthless. Other days, we think we're the best thing since sliced bread. (There's even a term to describe the cognitive bias where people who aren't actually very skilled have a tendency to think they're better than they are: *the Dunning-Kruger effect*.)

Calibration matters because it doesn't do me any good to think that I'm one thing when the world views me as another. For example, if I believe I'm an amazing public speaker but everyone else thinks my talks are tedious, I might make a bad decision like choosing to present a bold new idea myself instead of asking someone who would sell it better. Even worse, people will start to discount what I say because they'll conclude that I have a warped sense of reality.

To develop our self-awareness and to calibrate our strengths and weaknesses, we must confront the truth of what we're really like by asking others for their unvarnished opinions. The goal isn't to seek praise; the goal is to give our peers a safe opening where they can be honest—even brutally honest—so that we can get the most accurate information. In the same way that you gather feedback for your reports, you can learn about yourself through the following tactics:

- Ask your manager to help you calibrate yourself through the following two questions:

  What opportunities do you see for me to do more of what I do well? What do you think are the biggest things holding me back from having greater impact?

  What skills do you think a hypothetical perfect person in my role would have? For each skill, how would you rate me against that ideal on a scale of one to five?

- Pick three to seven people whom you work closely with and ask if they'd be willing to share some feedback to help you improve. Even if your company already has a process for 360-degree feedback, it helps to be specific about what you want to know and to provide reassurances that you're looking for honesty, not just pats on the back. Take the example below.

  Hey, I value your feedback and I'd like to be a more effective team member. Would you be willing to answer the questions below? Please be as honest as you can because that's what will help me the most—I promise nothing you say will offend me. Feedback is a gift, and I'm grateful for your taking the time.

  Examples of specific asks:

  On our last project together, in what ways did you see me having impact? What do you think I could have done to have more impact?

  With my team, what am I doing well that you'd like to see me do more of? What should I stop doing?

  One of the things I'm working on is being more decisive. How do you think I'm doing on that? Any suggestions on how I can do better here?

- Ask for task-specific feedback to calibrate yourself on specific skills. For example, if you're not sure how good of a public speaker you are, follow up with a few people after you give a presentation and say, "I'm hoping to improve my speaking skills. What do you think went well with my presentation? What would have made it twice as good?"

I'll pause here and acknowledge that asking for feedback is hard. You might have read the suggestions above and cringed when thinking about doing them.

It took me years before I got comfortable asking for feedback from others (outside of formal reviews where I had to). Why? It goes back to the imposter syndrome. Because I constantly worried that I wasn't good enough, I shied away from doing anything that might confirm that view. I imagined someone I respected telling me that yes, indeed, I wasn't doing X or Y very well. They've found me out! So I'd keep my mouth shut and soldier on, pretending that everything was fine.

It takes a certain amount of confidence to ask for critical feedback. For me, the breakthrough came when I realized I needed to change my mindset. If I saw every challenge as a test of my worthiness, then I'd constantly worry about where I stood rather than how I could improve. It's like stressing out more about your exam grade than about whether you're actually learning the concepts being taught.

On the other hand, if I approached challenges with the belief that I could get better at anything if I put in the effort, then the vicious cycle of anxious self-evaluation would be broken. No matter how good or bad I am at any particular skill, the notion that it's within my power to improve has allowed me to approach learning with curiosity instead of apprehension. And the rewards have been tremendous—I would never have known that my feedback was often vague and hand-wavy had I not invited that comment from a colleague. Once I heard it, I was able to work on making my points more precise and actionable, and now that's praised as one of my strengths.

In her influential book *Mindset*, pioneering psychologist Carol Dweck describes how the two different mindsets—which she calls *fixed* and *growth*—make a huge difference in our performance and personal happiness. Observe the difference:

SCENARIO: After completing an assignment, your manager gives you a few suggestions for improvement.

FIXED MINDSET: *Ugh, I really messed that up. My manager must think I'm an idiot.*

GROWTH MINDSET: *I'm thankful my manager gave me those tips. Now all my future assignments are going to go better.*

———

SCENARIO: You're asked if you'd like to take the lead on a risky and challenging new project.

FIXED MINDSET: *I'd better say no. I don't want to fail and embarrass myself.*

GROWTH MINDSET: *This is a great opportunity to stretch, learn something new, and gain the experience needed to lead other big projects down the road.*

———

SCENARIO: You've just had a tense 1:1 with your report Alice.

FIXED MINDSET: *I should act as if that went well so I come off like I know what I'm doing.*

GROWTH MINDSET: *I should ask Alice how she felt about that conversation and how we might have more productive discussions in the future.*

——

SCENARIO: You're in the middle of working on a proposal, and John asks to see your progress.

FIXED MINDSET: *I don't want to show John anything right now because the proposal is in rough shape. It'll make me look bad.*

GROWTH MINDSET: *John's feedback will be really helpful. In fact, I should share my early thinking with even more people so I can get ahead of any potential issues.*

The perspective you have changes everything. With a fixed mindset, your actions are governed by fear—fear of failure, fear of judgment, fear of being found out as an imposter. With a growth mindset, you're motivated to seek out the truth and ask for feedback because you know it's the fastest path to get you where you want to go.

UNDERSTAND YOURSELF AT YOUR BEST AND WORST

Beyond strengths and weaknesses, the next part of understanding yourself is knowing which environments help you to do your best work and which situations trigger a negative reaction. This helps you design your day-to-day to respond to your needs.

Over the years, here's what I've learned about what enables me to be my best:

- I've received at least eight hours of sleep the night before.
- I've done something productive early in the day, which motivates me to keep the momentum going.
- I know what my desired outcome looks like before I start.
- I have trust and camaraderie with the people I work with.

- I'm able to process information alone (and through writing) before big discussions or decisions.
- I feel like I'm learning and growing.

Once I understood those facts, I was able to change a few habits to make it easier for me to operate in my ideal environment. Here are some examples:

- I set up multiple "prepare for bed" alarms at 10:00 p.m., 10:15 p.m., and 10:30 p.m. so that my head can hit the pillow at 11:00 p.m. sharp.
- I exercise for ten to fifteen minutes in the morning right after I wake up. It's not much, but it gives me a sense of accomplishment that anchors the rest of the day.
- I schedule half an hour of "daily prep" into my calendar so I can study my day and visualize how I want each meeting or work task to go.
- I make an effort to become friends with my colleagues and learn about their lives outside of work.
- I schedule "thinking time" blocks on my calendar so I can sort through and write down my thoughts on big problems.
- Twice a year, I look back on the past six months and reflect on what I've gotten better at. Then, I set new learning goals for the next six months.

These little habits have given me a greater sense of control. They're not perfect by any means—even with adequate sleep and exercise I still end some days feeling drained. Meetings and tasks don't always go the way I plan. Sometimes, days (or weeks) will pass when my "thinking time" gets whittled to nothing. But these steps, as small as they are, make a difference in how well I work and think.

Other people have entirely different preferences for what helps them do their best work. One of my friends is a morning person—she wakes up every day at 5:00 a.m. and her first few hours of the day are her most productive. She tackles her hardest problems then and saves the less intensive tasks for the afternoon. Another friend tries to arrange his calendar so that he has to do as little context switching as possible. All his meetings and calls are chunked together back-to-back so that he can have long, uninterrupted blocks before and after.

If you're not sure what your ideal environment looks like, ask yourself the following:

- Which six-month period of my life did I feel the most energetic and productive? What gave me that energy?
- In the past month, what moments stand out as highlights? What conditions enabled those moments to happen, and are they re-creatable?
- In the past week, when was I in a state of deep focus? How did I get there?

The flip side of the coin is understanding which situations do the opposite—that is, they trigger an intensely negative reaction that derails your effectiveness. What separates triggers from normal negative reactions is that they have an outsize effect on *you* specifically. For example, any manager would feel disappointed if a promising candidate turned down an offer or if a star employee handed in a resignation letter. The more interesting question is: What are the things that push *your* buttons, but maybe not someone else's? That's when you're most at risk of being seen as irrational.

One of my triggers, for instance, is injustice. If something doesn't seem fair, my blood pressure rises and my heart starts to pound. I'll make a mountain out of a molehill by stubbornly arguing the point with others, even if I don't have all the information.

As you might guess, this doesn't always lead to the most productive discussions.

By knowing what triggers you, you can catch yourself in the moment and take a step back before responding like a hothead. If I take even five minutes to calm down, I'm back to being even-keeled.

It's helpful to share your triggers and learn what other people's are. Because we're all wired differently, your peers may not be aware of how their behavior is affecting you, and vice versa.

I once had a colleague who would speak on behalf of his entire team in executive reviews, including areas beyond his expertise. My fairness trigger would flare whenever he opened his mouth. *It seems really inconsiderate of him to not have his teammates speak to their areas of expertise*, I thought. When I privately told him this, he looked surprised but thanked me for the feedback. It had never occurred to him that he might come off as trying to take credit for others' work. He thought he was helping the review run more efficiently. Afterward, he made it a practice to shine the spotlight on others whenever he could.

Some people are triggered by those who come off as arrogant or self-serving. Others get antsy when a tiny detail isn't perfect. Maybe you recoil when someone says something in an aggressive or overly dramatic manner, or your temper flares when a team member takes days to respond to your messages.

Triggers occupy the space between your growth area and somebody else's—you could work on controlling your reactions, but the other person could also benefit from hearing your feedback.

To figure out what your triggers are, ask yourself the following questions:

- When was the last time someone said something that annoyed me more than it did others around me? Why did I feel so strongly about it?

- What would my closest friends say my pet peeves are?
- Who have I met that I've immediately been wary of? What made me feel that way?
- What's an example of a time when I've overreacted and later regretted it? What made me so worked up in that moment?

Knowing what lifts you up or brings you down is enormously valuable. Like how athletes have structured diet and exercise regimens to keep them competing in peak condition, the work you do to help yourself operate at your best will lead to many more winning days on the job.

FINDING YOUR CONFIDENCE WHEN YOU'RE IN THE PIT

No matter the twists and turns of your managerial road, on some days you will feel the imposter syndrome so strongly that you might as well be stuck at the bottom of a dark, deep pit. Every manager I know is well acquainted with this place, where the scathing commentary of your inner critic echoes off the sheer walls, turning whispers into screams.

In the Pit, you feel so very alone. Doubt is your soundtrack and fear is your sustenance. You second-guess every decision as you search desperately for something solid to grasp. All you want is faith restored—that you'll know where to go and what you should do. But you just can't find a way out.

I found myself in the Pit when a new colleague and I started working together on an important initiative. Right from the start, we butted heads on the product strategy. Both of us were so convinced we were right that every decision felt like a giant wave crashing on the flimsy sandcastle of our working relationship. I remember us sending long emails back and forth about minor product details. Running through it all was an undercurrent of mistrust—accusations of: "You aren't listening," "You don't know what you're talking about," and "It's my decision, not yours."

I felt terrible. I knew our relationship needed to improve, but how? Was I the one in the wrong? Maybe I really didn't know what I was talking about.

Looking back on that time now, I can see that my doubts got the better of me. I learned a lot through that tough collaboration and emerged with a better tool kit for escaping the Pit. If you find yourself in that same place, read on for tips on how best to manage your mental state.

Don't Beat Yourself Up for Feeling Bad

One of the worst parts of being in the Pit is the double whammy of struggling with something *and* worrying about the fact that you're struggling with it. *Why is this even hard for me?* your internal critic might wail. *If I were smarter or braver or more talented, I'd be fine.* By feeling guilty about the way you feel, you're creating even more stress for yourself.

Recognize that everyone in the world goes through hard times, and give yourself permission to worry. Don't pay the double tax on your mental load. I've found two tactics that help: The first is conjuring up a public figure you admire, someone who seems to have the perfect life, and Googling "[person's name] struggle." There is always a story. It's a good reminder that being in the Pit is universal.

The second tactic is to admit that you're feeling bad. I'll take out a Post-it note and write, "I am super stressed out about X." That little act shifts my mindset from worrying about my worries to simply declaring them. Once I do that, I can start to make progress on addressing the root cause.

Repeat After Me: "The Story I Have in My Head Is Probably Irrational"

Remember how we're all biased? Part of the reason bias exists is that our brains are wired to take shortcuts so we can arrive at faster conclusions. That's why stereotypes exist. If you see a person wearing thick glasses shuffling along with a stack of textbooks, you might conclude that she's good at math, even if you have no concrete evidence.

This also happens with how we perceive events. When we gather a few data points, we'll try to construct a complete narrative around it despite not actually having all the facts. And when we're in the Pit, our story tends to be the worst-case scenario.

For example, let's say you've been struggling with imposter syndrome and you discover you were left out of a meeting. You might conclude: *I wasn't invited because my teammates don't think I'm valuable.*

This example is so common that I've had at least a dozen people come to me over the years with this concern. "Let's get to the bottom of this," I'll say. So I'll reach out to the meeting organizers and ask, "Hey, why wasn't X invited to this meeting?" These are the top responses I get back:

1. *I didn't want to waste X's time and make him feel obligated to attend.*

2. *I didn't realize X cared about the meeting topic.*

3. *It was an honest mistake.*

Only once has the answer been in the ballpark of "We didn't think X would be valuable." (It was phrased as "We were worried X's strong views would steer the conversation off course.")

The stories we tell ourselves from a few scant pieces of evidence are often flat-out wrong, especially when we're in the Pit. Nine times out of ten, the other person is not out to get you. Your co-workers don't think you're an idiot. And, yes, you deserve this job.

When a negative story takes hold of you, step back and question whether your interpretation is correct. Are there alternative views you're not considering? What can you do to seek out the truth?

Sometimes, just squaring your shoulders and asking, "Why wasn't I invited to that meeting?" gets you out of speculation and into clarification. Even if you're afraid of the answer, confronting reality is always better than spinning disaster in your head.

Close Your Eyes and Visualize

Brain imaging studies show that when we picture ourselves doing something, the same parts of our brain are engaged as if we were *actually* doing that activity. Why does this matter? Because we can trick ourselves into getting some of the benefits of an activity simply by closing our eyes and imagining it in our heads.

Australian psychologist Alan Richardson discovered that a group of basketball players who were instructed to visualize themselves making free throws every day but who did not physi-cally practice did almost as well as another group who practiced shooting free throws for twenty minutes a day. Another study compared people who went to the gym every day with people who imagined themselves working out. The group who went to the gym every day increased their muscle strength by 30 percent; the group who ran through the workout in their heads increased their strength by 13.5 percent—almost half the benefit!

The legendary golfer Jack Nicklaus once wrote, "I never hit a shot, even in practice, without having a very sharp, in-focus pic-ture of it in my head. It's like a color movie."

Not only can visualization improve your outcomes, it can also help you find confidence when you're in the Pit. If you're feeling stuck, here are some exercises to try:

Imagine the anxiety, fear, and confusion you're feeling as not being personal to you, but universal things that everyone faces. One example I think of is Sheryl Sandberg admitting in her book *Lean In* that she was so worried what her colleagues might think of her leaving work at 5:00 p.m. that she'd sneakily exit the building when no one was watching. Another example is Reese Witherspoon confessing that she almost didn't accept an offer to be an ambassador of women's issues because she was terrified of giving speeches in front of large audiences. Both of these women are incredibly successful and inspiring role models. And yet, they face the same doubts I do because these emotions are perfectly human.

Imagine yourself succeeding wildly at something you're nervous about. Got a big presentation tomorrow? Imagine yourself walking into the room and flashing a smile at the audience. Picture yourself standing tall and speaking with poise. See the crowd attentive and nodding along as someone asks a hard question and you answer it confidently. The key to successful visualization is to make the scene as specific as possible.

Imagine a time in the past when you took on a hard challenge and knocked it out of the park. Now step through that entire experience in vivid detail. Remember how daunting that challenge first seemed? Walk through how you approached the problem. Recall the moment you realized you were going to be fine. Linger in particular on that feeling of success at the very end—the pride you felt, the compliments you received, the confidence you gained.

Imagine a room full of your favorite people telling you what they love about you. Picture them gathered in a circle, each person going turn by turn and pouring out their love and admiration for you. I like to go back to the speeches from family and friends on my wedding day, remembering how wonderful it felt to bask in their affection.

Imagine what your day would feel like if you were out of the Pit. Close your eyes and run through each hour on your calendar. Focus on the mental state you'd like to be in—for example, energetic during your morning workout, full and satisfied after your scrambled egg breakfast, friendly as you enter the office saying hello to people, engaged during your first meeting, etc.

Visualization is a powerful tool that doesn't require much—only a few minutes and a quiet spot to relax. Develop the habit to give yourself a boost of self-assurance for whatever comes your way.

Ask for Help from People You Can Be Real With

For years, when I found myself in the Pit, I bit my lip and kept it to myself. As the saying goes, "Fake it till you make it," so I thought that by pretending I had everything under control, I'd eventually stop feeling like a fraud, and nobody would be the wiser.

That line of thinking was a mistake. I denied myself the relief that comes from being able to share my fears with people I trust, and I missed out on their empathy and advice.

Admitting your struggles and asking for help is the opposite of weakness—in fact, it shows courage and self-awareness. You are saying that you care more about getting yourself to a good place than you do about your ego. When others understand our plight, we benefit tremendously. Research suggests that support groups are remarkably effective, even for serious mental health conditions. In one example, 82 percent of people with manic-depressive disorder reported coping better with their illness after joining a self-help group.

I've experienced this firsthand as well—a few years ago, I formed a Lean In Circle with a dozen other women at the company. Two hours every month, we'd go around the room and share what we were each grappling with—difficult relationships, uncertainty about our careers, struggles to balance parenthood with work. Tears were not uncommon because some of the challenges were truly hard. But I will never forget the warmth and camaraderie and how much that support meant to us. Where we could, we gave each other help and advice, and where we couldn't, we'd still offer our hugs and sympathetic ears.

Whether it's with your family, your best friend, a coach, or a group of trusted colleagues, find your support group. Use them as your cheerleaders and sounding board. No (wo)man is an island, and our community can light a path and lend a hand for us in our climb out of the Pit.

Celebrate the Little Wins

When you're in the Pit, you constantly pore over your failures because you're questioning whether or not you have what it takes to succeed. One way to break out of that negative cycle is to tell yourself a different story. Instead of thinking, *What am I not doing well?*, focus on all the ways you're winning.

During a particularly difficult period at work, I shared with a colleague how underwater I felt—I couldn't hire fast enough to keep up with all the projects that needed design leadership, so every day I felt the pressure of being the bottleneck. She reminded me that as tough as things were, not everything I was doing was a failure. In fact, one of my recent blog posts had really struck a chord with her, and she'd shared it with her entire team. "We got a lot out of it," she said, "so thank you for writing it."

Her words left a big impression. I realized I had come to view my writing as well as the many other responsibilities I had— reviewing design work, coaching, operational planning—as routine rather than valuable.

Inspired by that conversation, I started a journal called *Little Wins*. Every day, I'd jot down something I did that I was proud of, even if it was small. Sometimes, I'd celebrate a 1:1 where I gave someone helpful advice. Other days, I gave myself credit for running a productive meeting. Once, on a particularly tough day, I wrote down that I had managed to respond promptly to a few emails.

Studies show that if you write down five things you're grateful for every night, you'll feel happier in the long run. When you need to build your confidence, remember to do the same by focusing on all the things that you are doing well.

Practice Self-Care by Establishing Boundaries

When your work life overwhelms you, it can easily seep into everything. Maybe you're so stressed out about a project that you end up working nights and weekends. Or you can't stop thinking about your to-do list even when the rest of the world is asleep.

Resist this. Set boundaries by carving out time for the other important aspects of your life—spending time with loved ones, pursuing hobbies, exercising, giving back to your community, etc. In study after study, high workplace stress has been shown to inhibit creativity, whereas "when people were feeling more positive, they were more likely to be creative," says Teresa Amabile, Harvard Business School professor and author of *The Progress Principle*.

In my busiest periods, one exercise I turn to is scheduling a fifteen-minute activity at the beginning and end of the day that isn't related to work. I'll watch a TED Talk, play an iPhone game, do a crossword puzzle, exercise, or read. It's not a lot of time, but it helps me draw a line in the sand that says, "No matter what, I'll always make some time for me."

You can't do your best work unless you physically feel your best, so take care of yourself. It's always worth it.

LEARNING TO BE TWICE AS GOOD

Five years ago, I remember lying in bed at 3:00 a.m. before a big talk. My mind was furiously racing through the slides. My stomach was lurching like I was sailing on a storm-ridden sea. I thought of my favorite speakers and wondered how they did it. How amazing it must be, I thought, to waltz up in front of hundreds of people and feel genuinely excited instead of terrified. To actually *sleep* the night before and not worry about covering up under-eye circles the next day.

Fast-forward to this year. I'm lounging backstage at a conference an hour before I'm scheduled to present in front of thousands. Another speaker in the room paces back and forth, fidgeting with a notecard as he recites the opening lines to his talk. At one point he looks at me, smiles weakly, and says, "You look as cool as a cucumber." It was a tremendous compliment. And he was right—I wasn't nervous at all. My sleep the night before was long and luxurious. And I *was* genuinely excited!

So what happened in those years? Did I undergo intense speaker training? Did I become a PowerPoint and Keynote guru?

Did a little fairy whisper into my ear an amazing new method to calm my nerves?

The answer is predictably boring. I practiced and got better. There were years of stammering awkwardly in front of my team during weekly meetings. There were panels and talks I'd sign up to do even though I knew I'd dread it the night before. There were press interviews and Q&As, roundtables and TV appearances. Each one made the next a tad bit easier.

Management is a highly personal journey. We are all at different points on our path. Some of us start out stronger at certain skills than others. I was an introvert with a tendency to freeze up or ramble in front of large groups. I'm no exceptional orator today, but I've come a long way in both my skills and my confidence.

How you can be most effective will depend a lot on you: your strengths and growth areas, your personality and values. It will also depend on your organization's goals and culture—a small lemonade stand with a few employees needs different things than a large organization with tens of thousands of people.

The nature of this individual path means that most of your learning will happen on the job. Whether you need to improve your communication, get better at execution, become more strategic, or work better with others, set a lofty goal for yourself: *How can I be twice as good?* Then maximize your learning through the following.

Ask for Feedback

After an entire chapter on the importance of giving feedback to your reports, surely this comes as no surprise: if there is a secret sauce to self-improvement, it's to ask for feedback from other people *all the time*. The only hurdle you need to overcome is yourself—can you remember to ask frequently enough? Can you be humble and self-aware enough to hear it openly and then respond with real change?

Remember to ask for both task-specific and behavioral feedback. The more concrete you are about what you want to know, the better. If you lead with, "Hey, how do you think my presentation went?" you'll probably hear responses like "I think it went well," which aren't particularly helpful. Instead, probe at the specifics and make it easy for someone to tell you something actionable. "I'm working on making sure my point is clear in the first three minutes. Did that come across? How can I make it clearer next time?"

Always thank people for feedback. Even if you don't agree with what's said, receive it graciously and recognize that it took effort to give. If others find you defensive, you'll get less feedback in the future, which will only hurt your growth.

Treat Your Manager as a Coach

Given what we've discussed about the role of managers, your own boss should be one of your best sources of learning. But this might not naturally be the case. Maybe he doesn't see the day-to-day of your work, or he's busy putting out other fires, or he simply isn't as proactive about helping to guide your path as you'd like.

Regardless, the person most invested in your career isn't him; it's *you*. Your own growth is in your hands, so if you feel you aren't learning from your manager, ask yourself what you can do to get the relationship that you want.

One of the biggest barriers I've found is that people shy away from asking their managers for help. I know that feeling well; for years, I held the mental model that my boss—like my teachers and professors of the past—was someone in a position of authority who took note of what I did and passed judgment on it. As such, how I interacted with my manager could be summarized in one neat statement: *Don't mess it up*. I considered it a failure if my manager had to get involved in something I was responsible for. It felt to me like the equivalent of a blinking neon sign that read, *Warning: employee not competent enough to take care of task on her own.*

But we know by now that a manager's job is to help her team get better results. When you do better, by extension, she does better. Hence, your manager is someone who is on your side, who wants you to succeed, and who is usually willing to invest her time and energy into helping you. The key is to treat your manager as a coach, not as a judge.

Can you imagine a star athlete trying to hide his weaknesses from his coach? Would you tell a personal trainer, "Oh, I'm pretty fit, I've got it under control," when she asks you how she can help you achieve a better workout? Of course not. That is not how a coaching relationship works.

Instead, engage your manager for feedback. Ask, "What skills do you think I should work on in order to have more impact?" Share your personal goals and enlist his help: "I want to learn to become a better presenter, so I'd be grateful if you kept an eye out for opportunities where I can get in front of others." Tell him your hard problems so he can help you work through them: "I'm making a hiring call between two candidates with different strengths. Can I walk you through my thinking and get your advice?"

When I started to see 1:1s with my manager as an opportunity for focused learning, I got so much more out of it. Even when I'm not grappling with a problem, asking open-ended questions like, "How do you decide which meetings to attend?" or "How do you approach selling a candidate?" takes advantage of my manager's know-how and teaches me something new.

Make a Mentor Out of Everyone

There's no rule that says you can have only one coach. In fact, the world is full of people who can teach us. That's what a mentor is—someone who shares her expertise to help you improve. It doesn't need to be more formal than that. Sheryl Sandberg, in her book *Lean In*, cautions against treating the notion of a mentor as something too precious. Nobody wants to be asked, "Will you be my mentor?" because it sounds needy and time-consuming. But ask for *specific* advice instead, and you'll find tons of people willing to help.

In particular, people in your peer group—those with a similar job to yours—can be an excellent source of support and advice. I have a group of design manager friends whom I see every few months. Because we have similar responsibilities, we can discuss trends in the market, commiserate over shared challenges, and swap advice on how we handle critiques or host workshops.

One of these friends is a fantastic culture builder. She is able to cultivate a sense of warmth, camaraderie, and caring on her team that I really admire. Over the years, I've asked her dozens of questions on how she does it—how does she run her meetings? What tools does she use to communicate with her broader team? How does she manage to extend that sense of connection across remote offices? Her answers have directly shaped how I run my team. For example, I hold weekly office-hour blocks as a result of a direct tip from her.

Even when they don't have the same job as you, the people you work with probably all have something valuable to teach you. Maybe one colleague is an exceptional recruiter. Maybe another is really good at selling her ideas. Maybe your report is the most creative person you know. Maybe your manager has a keen ability to spot the best in everyone.

Whatever the skill, don't be afraid to ask, "Hey, I'm really impressed with the way you [do X]. I'd love to learn from you. Would you be willing to grab a coffee with me and share your approach?"

Keep in mind that since you're asking for a favor, it's well within people's rights to say no because they're busy or unsure of how to help. Thank them anyway. But more often than you might think, the answer will be yes. We've all benefited from the mentorship of others, so many people are happy to pay it forward.

Set Aside Time to Reflect and Set Goals

When you're racing full steam ahead and the scenery is zooming past you, it's hard to comprehend the entirety of your journey. Where did you start? How far is there to go? Which parts were smooth and which were filled with potholes?

A study from Harvard Business School shows that we learn more when we couple our experiences with periodic reflections. Even though people prefer to learn by doing, "participants who chose to reflect outperformed those who chose additional experience."

Reflection doesn't have to be some kind of heavy process. At the end of the day, you're doing it for your own benefit, so find what works best for you. Personally, I like to schedule an hour on my calendar at the end of every week to think about what I accomplished, what I'm satisfied or dissatisfied with, and what I'm taking away for next week. I then jot down some notes in an email to my team, as an easy way to keep up the habit.

I also set personal goals and do bigger look-backs every six months, which gives me a longer time frame to tackle ambitious projects and learn new skills.

Here are examples of what my one-week and six-month notes look like:

THOUGHTS ON MY WEEK:

- *Recent feedback I heard: Through my Q&As, I'm hearing a lot of praise for our design team culture, which is awesome. On what we could be doing better, the top theme was clarifying expectations for career growth. I'm taking away that we need to get more buttoned-up on how we talk about assessing performance and promotions.*

- *Recruiting for next year: In our planning meeting, remote office growth came up as a big theme. We will need to train more interviewers and make sure our debriefs are consistent across offices. I'm counting on all of us to be heavily involved, and we're getting a plan together for what that looks like.*

- *Strategy for Project X: I worked with Team Y to prepare our proposals for the upcoming review. This came a long way in a few short weeks—shout-out to Elena in particular for her great work here.*

- *Understanding research needs: In my 1:1s, I've been hearing asks for more research involvement. I have a better sense of what we're looking for now, and David and I will share a staffing plan in the next two weeks.*

GOALS FOR THE NEXT SIX MONTHS:

- *Build out my bench: Fill three open roles to ensure that every product has a strong leader.*

- *Evolve all product reviews to start with clearly defined people problems so we have a common basis for evaluation.*

- *Become an expert in hiring great research leaders.*

- *Get rid of status updates in my 1:1s: Use that time to have deeper conversations with my reports.*

- *Don't bring work home with me: Focus on being more efficient in the office.*

At the end of every six months, I'll pull up my goals and evaluate how I did. The important thing isn't the grade but what I learned. If I didn't succeed at getting everyone to frame their work differently, why was that? Were my tactics ineffective? Did I not communicate things clearly? Were they simply not important?

If I did hit a goal—say, hiring three strong leaders—there are lessons to be had as well. What allowed me to be successful? Would I be able to take on even more ambitious goals in the future, say, hiring five leaders? What tips might I give to someone else looking to do the same thing?

The more your experiences—good or bad—get shaped into lessons and stories that help you and others, the faster your growth trajectory.

Take Advantage of Formal Training

If you have the opportunity to get formal training, take it. This might mean signing up for a company seminar, attending an industry conference, participating in a roundtable discussion, hearing experts on a panel, or engaging in a hands-on workshop.

It might seem obvious that formal training is helpful, but it also rarely feels urgent or necessary. Besides costing time, it also tends to cost money, which means we engage in a classic back-and-forth with ourselves: *Is it worth it?* Especially in the middle of a hectic week, is it really a good idea to step away for a two-day workshop or to give up a relaxing evening at home for a lecture?

The answer is usually yes. If spending ten hours being trained helps you be even 1 percent more efficient at your job, then it's a good return on investment (1 percent of time saved per year is about twenty hours).

I remember taking a one-day class several years ago on how to have hard conversations. Those eight hours transformed the way I approached conflict. I left with a newfound belief that, yes, it *is* possible to have a productive conversation with anyone about anything. Even now, not a single week goes by where I don't call to mind something I took away from that course.

Another type of formal training is professional coaching. You will likely need to pay for this out of pocket unless your company covers it (some do for senior-level employees). Many CEOs and executives work with professional coaches because, at that level, there are fewer people who can naturally serve as mentors, and even small improvements in performance translate to significant impact for the organization.

When you think about formal training, the question to ask isn't *Is this worth doing right now given all the other things on my plate (or all the other things I could spend money on)*, but rather *One year from now, will I be happy I did this?* When framed that way, the choice tends to be clearer.

When you invest in your personal learning and growth, you're not just investing in your own future but also the future of your team. The better you are, the more you're able to support others.

———

New managers sometimes ask me, "A decade into the job, what's something you're still continuing to learn?" My answer is, "How to be the best leader I can while staying true to who I am."

Managers so often think of the role as being in service to something else—the mission of the organization, the goals of the team, the needs of others—that it's easy to forget about the most important character in your management journey: *you.*

Learning how to be a great leader means learning about your superpowers and flaws, learning how to navigate the obstacles in your head, and learning how to learn. With these tools comes the confidence that you're meant to be here just as you are—no masks or pretenses needed—and that you're ready for whatever challenges lie ahead.

Chapter Six

Amazing Meetings

As my team grew, I thought it would be a good idea to host a meeting where everyone went around the room and shared what they were up to that week. I had seen other managers run similar status or "stand-up" meetings, and I thought this was standard practice for keeping folks in the loop about what was going on.

The idea was better in theory than in practice; what I hadn't accounted for was the variation in how people described their work. Some kept it short and sweet, while others went into extreme detail about the email debates they got into with their engineers on Thursday nights. After a few months, it became clear that this meeting was the work equivalent of a history teacher droning on about some battle in the year 1752. All around me, I saw glazed eyes and heard keyboard *tap-tap-tap*s from those who figured their time was better spent doing other work.

After one such session, I was greeted with an email in my inbox from a team member asking if I had ever considered asking everyone to send out email updates instead of waxing poetic in person. "To be honest, this meeting doesn't feel like a good use of time," it concluded.

Gutsy move, telling your manager her meeting sucks. But the feedback was spot-on. I canceled the series, and we went to weekly email updates, which worked out beautifully. I left with a deeper appreciation of both the importance of planning good meetings and the value of giving feedback to improve bad meetings.

I think about meetings a lot because it's such a huge part of what

I do. The majority of my day is spent with different sets of people in 1:1s, small groups, larger groups, and, occasionally, audiences of hundreds or thousands.

Meetings tend to have a bad rap, like they're the "necessary evil" of management or the grown-up equivalent of homework. They're parodied as wasteful, bureaucratic, and boring, though nobody seems to be able to get rid of them entirely. And we spend a lot of time in them. A 2011 study found that, on average, chief executives spend 60 percent of their time in meetings, with another 25 percent spent on calls or at public events. Another study analyzed a single executive meeting at a large company and found that, all told, it took 300,000 person-hours to prep for—a staggering number!

Leo Tolstoy begins *Anna Karenina* with the statement "Happy families are all alike; every unhappy family is unhappy in its own way." Meetings are much the same. Think of all the bad meetings you have attended—the room argued in circles; you went in for clarity and left with confusion; the attendees felt disengaged; the content shared was repetitive; the group veered sharply off course from the agenda; an individual or two dominated the room and nobody else could get a word in; and so on.

On the other hand, good meetings are simple and straightforward. You leave them feeling the same way every time:

- The meeting was a great use of my time.
- I learned something new that will help me be more effective at my job.
- I left with a clearer sense of what I should do next.
- Everyone was engaged.
- I felt welcomed.

At the end of the day, talking with someone face-to-face is still one of the best ways to communicate and get work done. As a manager, you will attend countless meetings as well as run many of your own. Take the responsibility seriously and don't perpetuate bad meeting culture. Instead, steer the precious time you and your colleagues spend together toward what's truly valuable.

WHAT IS A GREAT OUTCOME FOR YOUR MEETING?

You may hear the conventional wisdom that "all meetings should have a purpose." That's good advice, but it doesn't go far enough. My status meeting had a purpose—keep everyone informed about the team's weekly progress. It still ended up lousy because I didn't ask myself, *What does a great outcome look like?*

If I had, I would have realized that what I really wanted was for the members of the team to feel closer to each other and collaborate more effectively. Clearly, if people were tuning out, I wasn't succeeding.

There are only a handful of reasons for people to get together in person, so being crystal clear about the outcome you're shooting for is the first step to running great meetings.

Making a Decision

In a decision meeting, you're framing the different options on the table and asking a decision-maker to make a call.

Success here is both getting to a clear decision *and* everyone leaving with a sense of trust in the process. You don't need consensus, but those whom the decision affects should feel that the way it was made was efficient and fair.

If people don't trust the process, you'll find that the decision drags on. Here's an example of how I used to fall into this trap:

REPORT: *Right now we're looking at a deadline to finish our design work by next Tuesday. This is a problem because it isn't enough time to explore the three options we talked about. Are you supportive of us moving the deadline back by a week?*

ME: *Makes sense. I am supportive.*

Do you see the problem? I just made a decision, but I heard only one piece of context—that my report felt there wasn't enough time to adequately do the work. But what are the consequences of moving the deadline back? Here's what would happen next:

ENGINEERING MANAGER: *Hey, I just heard that you okayed our moving the design milestone back. This is a problem because I have a team of seven engineers who are waiting for the designs to be finalized, and pushing things back means we're not going to have enough time to hit the engineering milestone. Can we go back to the original timeline?*

Now I'm stuck between a rock and a hard place. The engineering team is mad because they felt that I made a decision without hearing their side of the story. They want me to remake the decision with new information. But if I do that and change my call, my report is going to be frustrated. I've just lost myself some major credibility. The best thing I can do now is admit that I made a mistake with my process and gather everyone for a do-over on the decision.

"But wait a minute," you might say. "The two sides disagree, so any decision made is going to leave someone unhappy."

I challenge that notion. Everyone on a team ultimately shares the same goals. In this case, both designers and engineers want to ship a great experience as soon as possible. While people may have different opinions about the best path to take, part of working well together is placing trust in decision-makers and in a fair process. As Amazon CEO Jeff Bezos is fond of saying, sometimes you have to "disagree and commit" for the sake of moving forward quickly.

A great decision-making meeting does the following:

- Gets a decision made (obviously)
- Includes the people most directly affected by the decision as well as a clearly designated decision-maker
- Presents all credible options objectively and with relevant background information, and includes the team's recommendation if there is one
- Gives equal airtime to dissenting opinions and makes people feel that they were heard

Here are some examples of bad outcomes to avoid:

- People feel that their side wasn't presented well, so they don't trust the resulting decision.
- Decisions take a long time to make, which delays progress. While important and hard-to-reverse decisions deserve deep consideration, be wary of spending too much time on small, easy-to-reverse decisions.
- Decisions keep flip-flopping back and forth, which makes it hard to trust and act on them.
- Too much time is spent trying to get a group to consensus rather than escalating quickly to a decision-maker.
- Time is wasted on rehashing the same argument twenty different ways.

Sharing Information

We all need information to do our jobs well, whether it's the CEO's vision, the latest sales figures, the opinions of various stakeholders, or the timeline for a particular project. A few decades ago, meetings were the primary way groups of people shared and received information. Nowadays, with email and chat right at our fingertips, it's less necessary (and often less efficient) for in-person get-togethers solely focused on the transfer of knowledge.

Done well, however, there are a few big benefits of informational meetings over other channels like bulletin boards, mailing lists, or group posts. The first is that they allow for more interactivity. So, for example, if you want everyone to know about a potentially controversial policy change, sharing that news in person allows the group to ask questions or express their reactions.

The second benefit is that a well-prepared informational meeting is usually a lot more interesting than a bunch of words on a page. Eye contact, body language, and visible passion all help to make a message come alive.

Today, our design organization gets together periodically to highlight important work we're doing, share new tools and processes, and discuss lessons we've learned. Unlike my discontinued status meeting, this one works because there is a lot more preparation behind it to ensure the content is interesting.

A great informational meeting accomplishes the following:

- Enables the group to feel like they learned something valuable
- Conveys key messages clearly and memorably
- Keeps the audience's attention (through dynamic speakers, rich storytelling, skilled pacing, interactivity)
- Evokes an intended emotion—whether inspiration, trust, pride, courage, empathy, etc.

Providing Feedback

Often known as a "review," the purpose of a feedback meeting is for stakeholders to understand and give input on work in progress. Sometimes, this might end with an uneventful "this looks fine." Other times, the feedback can result in significant deviations from the plan.

It's tempting to judge success on whether or not the boss likes the work. This is a mistake. Feedback meetings don't exist to pass or receive judgment but rather to get to the best outcome. Gunning for approval creates incentives to focus more on the smoke and mirrors of the presentation than on getting the most helpful feedback to improve the work.

A great feedback meeting achieves the following:

- Gets everyone on the same page about what success for the project looks like
- Honestly represents the current status of the work, including an assessment of how things are going, any changes since the last check-in, and what the future plans are
- Clearly frames open questions, key decisions, or known concerns to get the most helpful feedback
- Ends with agreed-upon next steps (including when the next milestone or check-in will be)

Generating Ideas

You might hear this referred to as a "brainstorming meeting" or a "working session" where a group of people get together to come up with proposed solutions to a problem. Brainstorming was popularized in the 1950s by an advertising executive named Alex Osborn, who suggested that to get more out-of-the-box thinking, groups should focus on *maximizing the quantity of ideas* and *withholding judgment of those ideas*.

Unfortunately, having twelve people in a room blurt out whatever comes to mind isn't actually effective for innovation—we have a tendency to conform our new ideas to what's already been discussed or suggest fewer ideas because we assume other people are carrying the load.

The best idea generation comes from understanding that we need *both* time to think alone (because our brains are most creative when we're by ourselves) *and* time to engage with others (because hearing different perspectives creates sparks that lead to even better ideas).

Preparation and good facilitation is key. A great generative meeting does the following:

- Produces many diverse, nonobvious solutions through ensuring each participant has quiet alone time to think of ideas and write them down (either before or during the meeting)
- Considers the totality of ideas from everyone, not just the loudest voices
- Helps ideas evolve and build off each other through meaningful discussion
- Ends with clear next steps for how to turn ideas into action

Strengthening Relationships

To have a high-functioning team, people need to work well with one another, so you need to find ways to nurture empathy, create trust, and encourage collaboration. Sometimes, you may decide to get a group of people together for the simple purpose of focusing on relationships.

Team lunches, dinners, and other social events serve this purpose, as do some 1:1s and team meetings. When we all understand each other a little better as human beings—when we've invested time to learn about our colleagues' values, hobbies, families, life stories, etc.—then working together also becomes easier and more enjoyable.

A great team-bonding meeting isn't about the number of hours spent together or the lavishness of the event. Instead, it enables the following:

- Creates better understanding and trust between participants
- Encourages people to be open and authentic
- Makes people feel cared for

Every meeting should be clear on which of the above it's trying to accomplish. Don't try to make a single meeting do too much, and remind the group of its primary purpose when the conversation starts to deviate. For example, if you're looking for a decision on pricing, and people start chiming in with suggestions for new features, say that you'll separately find time to discuss the latter topic, and then steer the conversation back toward the intended agenda. In my experience, it's unlikely that the structure of a decision meeting makes it a good forum for generating ideas.

Practice clarity and ruthless efficiency with your meetings, and people will thank you for respecting the sanctity of their time.

INVITE THE RIGHT PEOPLE

You're more likely to have a great meeting if everyone necessary, and nobody extraneous, is there. We've all been in rooms with lackluster energy because there are too many people crowded around the table, many of them distracted and on their phones. Do they all need to be in attendance? Probably not.

I've also been in meetings where the goal was to make a decision that would have huge impact on some other team—for example, a product decision about which features to build also affects its sales prospects—but there weren't representatives from that other team present. This is costly as well because you can't make a fair decision without all affected stakeholders in the room, so either the decision gets delayed or it risks being reescalated and debated again.

How do you know whom you should invite? Go back to your answer for what a great outcome looks like for your meeting, and ask yourself: Which people are necessary to make that outcome happen?

Sometimes, reasonable people can disagree on who needs to be present. A while ago, I ran a review meeting where I and a few other managers gave feedback on the design work across my team. All the designers were invited. As we continued to hire more people, the number of attendees grew and grew until the meeting felt like a lecture hall. There were still only a handful of people presenting in each session, which meant everybody else was mainly watching and listening.

I suggested that we cut the attendance list, but not all the managers agreed. The meeting was useful, one person argued, because it exposed new designers to the kind of feedback they should expect. Furthermore, another manager added, it was a high-visibility meeting with lots of exposure to leadership, and to be in that room gave people the sense that they were valued members of the team.

These were excellent points. Yes, the meeting did serve an informational purpose in teaching what we valued in good design. It also did help create more connections to senior leaders. If I shrank the invite list to just those presenting, we'd lose those benefits.

But going back to the *primary* goal of the review, it was so I and other managers could give helpful feedback on projects in midflight. Having so many other observers made that harder. The atmosphere felt formal and high pressure. The presenters were starting to spend too much time tweaking the details of their Keynote decks. And as a reviewer, I felt I needed to choose my words carefully in front of such a big crowd, which meant I couldn't be as casual and direct as I would have liked.

Ultimately, we decided to shrink the attendee list. We resolved to find other ways to invest in design education and building relationships, including sharing a detailed write-up of the meeting notes and hosting more leadership Q&As. Folks on the team reclaimed a weekly hour, but more important, the review meeting went back to being lower pressure, more honest, and more effective at doing what it was meant to do.

GIVE PEOPLE A CHANCE TO COME PREPARED

In many a review, I'd be the person in the room with the perplexed expression, squinting at the charts and graphs projected in front of us while the presenters said things like, "So as you can clearly see from the data here . . ." *Wait, wait!* I wanted to yell. *I don't see how you got to that conclusion. . . . Am I just really slow?*

I've since learned that my reaction wasn't unusual and certainly nothing to be self-conscious about. Even my data-savviest colleagues need time to process new information.

Because the presenters knew their material forward and back, they experienced what social psychologists call "the curse of knowledge"—the cognitive bias that makes it difficult for them to remember what it's like to be a beginner seeing the content for the first time. That's why they assumed the room could quickly grasp all the salient points as they flipped from slide to slide.

But if the goal of the meeting is to make decisions or give feedback, it can be tough for stakeholders to understand the material well enough in the span of a single meeting to arrive at thoughtful conclusions.

The solution is to help everyone come prepared. The change we made to our decision and review meetings was to ask the organizers to send out any presentations or documents the day before so that everyone got the chance to process the information in advance. This meant that I could spend as much time as I needed to understand all the charts and graphs, which allowed me to be a better contributor in the meeting.

Sending out an agenda ahead of time shows a level of care and intentionality in helping the group stay focused. It's a good idea to do this for meetings of any size, even 1:1s, but the larger the meeting, the more important the preparation. If this sounds like a lot of work, consider the actual monetary cost of a given meeting.

If a company-wide meeting attended by five hundred employees isn't engaging or memorable, then the company will have wasted five hundred people-hours—ten thousand dollars if you assume a twenty-dollar-per-person hourly wage. Spending even five hours of five people's time (five hundred dollars total) to prepare for that meeting is undoubtedly worth it. Even one recurring weekly meeting with a handful of attendees can translate to thousands of dollars of wasted productivity over the course of a year if that time together isn't well spent.

After the meeting, the follow-ups need to be treated with as much care as the preparation. A single meeting is not an end unto itself; it is a stepping-stone in the much longer path of creating something valuable for the world.

In the last few minutes of a meeting, get into the habit of asking, "So before we break, let's make sure we agree on next steps . . ." After the meeting, send out a recap to the attendees with a summary of the discussion, a list of specific action items and who is responsible for each, and when the next check-in will be.

If a decision was made, then that should be communicated to the right people. If feedback was given, then that should be acted upon. If ideas were generated, then the meeting organizer should clarify what the process is to take those to the next stage. These follow-ups can then anchor the agenda for when the group reconvenes.

MAKE IT SAFE FOR PEOPLE TO CONTRIBUTE

Early in my career, I was the quiet person whose contributions in meetings were inversely proportional to how many people were in the room. Which meant that in 1:1s, I'd say a lot, but in groups over seven, I'd make like a ninja and stay as inconspicuous as possible.

After I became a manager, I saw this same phenomenon in many folks on my team. Not everyone is comfortable rattling off whatever's top of mind in front of a group. For me, it was fear of judgment—I worried that I would say something stupid and waste other people's time.

What helped me find my voice were environments that felt safe, supportive, and nonjudgmental. It was easier to share when I saw everyone else doing the same versus just one or two talkative people. Or, when somebody asked for my opinion because she was genuinely curious: "Julie, you haven't said anything yet— what do you think about this proposal?" Or when I had a good enough relationship with the other folks present to know that they wouldn't *actually* think I was incompetent, even if I said something stupid.

If you are a meeting organizer trying to generate ideas, make a decision, or create stronger relationships, you will get better results if you can get your entire group to contribute. This is why it's so important to foster a welcoming environment for questions, discussions, discourse, and dissent. If you present what you think is a brilliant idea but most of the room secretly thinks it's ridiculous, it doesn't help you if nobody feels comfortable telling you how they really feel. To avoid being the emperor with no clothes on, try the following.

Be Explicit about the Norms You Want to Set

If you want everyone to participate in your meeting, sometimes the easiest tactic is just to say that directly.

One of the things I do with my team is host regular Q&As. It's important to me that people feel they can ask me hard questions and get straight answers. However, after doing about a dozen of these, I noticed that I rarely got tough questions. People in the audience would look at each other, as if daring someone else to ask first.

It couldn't be because my team didn't have any hard questions— I'd often hear through the grapevine that folks were skeptical about a particular strategy or wondered why one of our initiatives wasn't going well. But they never came up in Q&A. Finally, I decided I should address the elephant in the room.

In the next meeting, I opened with this: "I'm here to do a Q&A because it's really important to me that we can have real talk about all the things happening on our team. But to be honest, I don't get the sense that I'm hearing all of your top concerns. So I want to say this up front: Hard questions are good! Get them off your chest! I promise to be as transparent as I can."

That worked—by explicitly saying that I valued transparency and welcomed hard questions, many more people asked them.

Change Up Your Meeting Format to Favor Participation

An unstructured group discussion means that participants choose if and when they speak. If you have an introverted set of people, you might struggle with getting them to voice their thoughts. If you have extroverts, they might dominate the conversation. Differences in seniority, tenure, or familiarity also play a role in people's comfort in speaking up.

You can combat natural group dynamics by suggesting more structured approaches. One example is going around the room. If there is a decision to make among three options, you might ask every person which one he or she favors and why. This guarantees that no perspectives are left unsaid.

Another tactic I like is the "Post-it note" opening. Before launching into a discussion about a complex topic (for example, what our marketing goals should be or what success looks like three years from now), give everyone a pad of Post-it notes and ask them to write down their thoughts on the topic. Then, have the room work in quiet concentration for about ten to fifteen minutes.

Afterward, each participant puts his or her notes up on the board and talks through their thinking. Similar ideas are clumped together, and after the very last note has been added, the room discusses the various "clumps."

By encouraging people to get their own thoughts down on paper before sharing them, the barrier to participation is lowered.

Manage Equal Airtime

If your meetings tend to be dominated by a few individuals, try mediating the amount of airtime everyone gets.

Be on the lookout for interruptions. If someone starts making a point but another loud voice cuts her off, provide cover by saying, "Hang on, Ann wasn't finished." As an added bonus, I've found that doing this also bolsters your own credibility.

Similarly, if you see someone seeking to get a word in, you can help create an opening: "John looks like he wants to say something." My colleague did this for me once in an executive review with twenty other people, and to this day I remember the rush of gratitude I felt.

Particularly perceptive managers might even try directed questions: "Susan, you look puzzled—what do you think we should do?" or "Rick, we haven't heard from you yet. What's your opinion?"

For the overtalkers, be clear but polite in letting them know that it's time for someone else to get a turn: "Ian, it's clear you have more you want to say, but let's first make sure other people get a chance to weigh in" or "Laura, I'm hearing that you feel very strongly we should do X—before we wrap, does anyone have another opinion? I want to make sure all points of view are heard."

It's not always comfortable to interrupt others and manage the flow of conversation in this manner, but it sends a strong signal that you believe better outcomes come from hearing a diversity of perspectives.

Get Feedback about Your Meeting

If you're lucky, you'll have a candid team member who will tell you when he or she feels that your meeting is not a good use of time. However, there's a more reliable way: make a habit of asking for feedback, especially on recurring meetings with a larger audience.

Remember that the key to getting great feedback is being specific about what you want to know and making it safe for the person to tell you her honest opinion. Leading with what you suspect may be an issue signals that it's okay for the person to be critical.

With my failed status meeting, I could have asked: "How useful do you think my weekly status meeting is? My goal is to give everyone context on who's doing what so there's better collaboration and support across the team. But I wonder if it's too bogged down in the details right now. What do you think?"

Think back to the best meetings you've had. How did they feel? My favorites are the ones with a friendly and genuinely curious vibe. There isn't an invisible layer of tension or pressure hovering over us. People feel safe to toss out their crazy ideas or say, "I disagree." Everyone understands that their presence and contributions are appreciated. That's the kind of meeting we should aspire to run.

SOME MEETINGS DON'T NEED YOU AND SOME DON'T NEED TO EXIST AT ALL

Some years ago, during a particularly tough period at the office, I was regularly working past midnight on nights and weekends. *This isn't sustainable*, I thought to myself. *Why am I feeling so behind on everything?*

I told this to my husband and his first question was, "What does your calendar look like?" "Busy," I replied. "Back-to-back meetings." "Huh," he said. "Do you need to be in all of them?"

His words motivated me to take a deeper look at my schedule. For a week, I made a note of every meeting I attended and how I felt at the end of it. Did I participate? Was I critical to the outcome? Did I get something meaningful out of being there in person?

At the end of the week, I was stunned to discover that for about 40 percent of my meetings, the answer was no. Truth be told, some meetings I attended because I wanted to feel in the know or simply because I was on the invite list and felt obligated to show up. But all that time could have been spent on the priorities that kept me up at night instead!

I thought my results were extreme, but I learned that they weren't unusual. Leslie Perlow of Harvard Business School and her colleagues surveyed 182 senior managers from a diverse set of companies. They found that 65 percent said meetings prevented them from completing their own work, 71 percent found their meetings unproductive and inefficient, and 64 percent said meetings come at the expense of deep thinking.

As a result of my audit, I went on a deep calendar cleanse. I purged myself of meetings I wasn't really contributing to. When I wanted to stay in the loop about relevant decisions, I asked the meeting organizers to include me on pre- and post-meeting notes. With the time I regained, I was able to get to a healthier balance and focus on doing a better job on the things I cared about.

As a manager, your time is precious and finite, so guard it like a dragon guards its treasure stash. If you trust that the right outcomes will happen without you, then you don't need to be there.

Be on the lookout as well for meetings that don't seem valuable for *anyone*. They should be canceled or revamped. Research by Nale Lehmann-Willenbrock and her colleagues found a direct connection between well-planned meetings (where the right people are invited, the agenda is organized, and the interactions are useful) and outcomes like team performance and employee well-being. Bad meetings can "leave employees feeling frustrated, and can also trigger employee exhaustion and potential burnout," Lehmann-Willenbrock says, whereas "good meetings can boost employee morale."

I used to have a meeting on Wednesdays that I dreaded going to because it felt so tense and confrontational. All the attendees sat with arms and legs crossed, like we were debating nuclear weapons policy instead of process improvements. Anything that was said was immediately refuted or met with a long period of silence. Thankfully, the meeting series eventually ended with a larger team reorganization.

Some years later, I was talking with a colleague who happened to be in that same meeting with me, and we both realized that we thought the meeting was a waste of time. Our group hadn't yet established trust with each other, so every debate felt high stakes and unproductive. "Why didn't we recognize that then and shut the meeting down earlier?" we asked ourselves. Lesson learned.

If you find yourself in a recurring meeting of questionable value, do everyone an important service by kindly letting the organizer know. Life's too short to be wasted in subpar meetings. Aim to make every single one you are a part of useful, awesome, and energizing so that your team can achieve more together.

Chapter Seven

Hiring Well

AVOID

ASPIRE

Early in my career, when interviewing other people still felt new and scary, I found myself face-to-face with a new grad candidate named Tom. He smiled shyly as I introduced myself. After I threw out my first interview problem, he grabbed a marker and began sketching out the solution on a whiteboard. I noticed that his hands were shaking slightly. He asked a few thoughtful questions. When he got stuck, he stopped, stepped back, and talked through his thoughts out loud.

By the end of our interview, he hadn't completely solved all the problems I'd posed. I could tell he was disappointed. I imagined him going home, pulling out a notebook, and continuing to plug away until he arrived at a solution. That's the kind of person he seemed to be.

Even though he didn't get as far as other candidates on my questions, when it came time to cast our decisions, I said, "Hire." This surprised even me. My default was to vote conservatively—if I had any hesitation about a candidate, it felt safer to say, "No hire." This was the first time I had ever gone out on a limb for someone. But I just couldn't shake the feeling that Tom was something special: not just smart but unusually dedicated and thoughtful. I knew I'd like working with him.

Fortunately, after some discussion with the other interviewers, we decided to give Tom an offer. A few years later, I saw him at a party. He came up to me and said, "You know, I still remember our interview. I was so nervous, and I didn't do very well on your problem. I was sure you weren't going to hire me."

I smiled and joked that I had a crystal ball that showed me just how awesome he'd be. Because Tom *was* awesome. After he joined, his trajectory was like a rocket ship's. In a few short years, he went from new grad to senior engineering leader. Even though we didn't work closely together, I often heard his name uttered through the grapevine, always with deep respect. He was incredibly smart, and yet he remained one of our most thoughtful and dedicated colleagues.

At a growing organization, hiring well is the single most important thing you can do. At this point, I've interviewed and helped bring in hundreds of people—more than the entirety of the company when I started! Those people have, in turn, gone on to bring in many more. If you had told me when I joined that I'd be one of the reasons why *thousands* of my coworkers are here today, I'd have thought you were crazy.

Hiring doesn't just matter at scale—even a single great hire can make a big difference in your team's outcomes.

The most important thing to remember about hiring is this: hiring is not a *problem* to be solved but an opportunity to build the future of your organization.

This lesson took me a while to learn. Because my team grew so rapidly, the need to hire was like an ever-present cloud looming over me. We never seemed to have enough people, so hiring felt like the thing I *had* to do to solve the problem of overstretched reports and understaffed projects. How could I put these fires out as quickly as possible?

And yet, hiring isn't just about filling holes. If you approach it that way, you're not going to bring in the best people. It's about figuring out how to make your team and your own *life* much, much better. In addition to contributing their talents, our favorite coworkers teach us new things, inspire and support us, and make going to work a whole lot more fun. Looking back now, I can't think of anything more satisfying than meeting someone for the first time, realizing how awesome they are, and working with them for years to come on meaningful problems.

At the same time, hiring well is hard. As they say in fairy tales, you'll have to meet a lot of frogs in order to find a good match. In this chapter, we'll discuss the best ways to approach building a great team.

DESIGN YOUR TEAM INTENTIONALLY

When you are buckling under the strain of a short-staffed team, it can be very hard to resist someone who seems available and ready to do the work. You might well overlook the fact that they aren't exactly what you want—similar to how, when your stomach is growling and you're raiding the fridge, pickles, ketchup, and bread seems like an acceptable meal.

The solution to both a healthier diet and a better team is to plan ahead. If you go to the grocery store on Sunday and buy what you need for a wholesome meal every night, then when hunger strikes Wednesday evening, you're more likely to reach for the chicken and veggies.

One exercise I do every January is to map out where I hope my team will be by the end of the year. I create a future org chart, analyze gaps in skills, strengths, or experiences, and make a list of open roles to hire for. You can do something similar by asking yourself the following questions:

- How many new people will I add to our team this year (based on company growth, expected attrition, budget, priorities, etc.)?
- For each new hire, what level of experience am I looking for?

- Which specific skills or strengths do we need in our team (for example, creative thinking, operational excellence, expertise in XYZ, etc.)?

- Which skills and strengths does our team already have that new hires can stand to be weaker in?

- What traits, past experiences, or personalities would strengthen the diversity of our team?

Having a thoughtful, one-year-out organizational plan lets you stay ahead of hiring needs and gives you a handy framework for evaluating candidates so that you won't fall into the trap of saying yes to the next person who comes along.

Even if things change—your organization restructures, an employee abruptly leaves, priorities shift—you can modify your plan as you go along so that there's always a clear picture in your head of what your team should look like.

This exercise will look a little different if you're at a company without a lot of hiring needs. In that case, the size and composition of your team a year from now might remain pretty similar to today. Still, it's useful to consider the possibility of attrition and where you'll look if someone on your team leaves. Where did your best employees come from? What new skills, if any, would you want to add? And who specifically might you love to bring on board if a spot opens up?

HIRING IS *YOUR* RESPONSIBILITY

If you have the good fortune of working with a dedicated recruiting team, you may be tempted to believe that you can lean back and expect top candidates to be delivered to your door.

Let me quickly disabuse you of that notion. No recruiter can possibly know what an ideal candidate looks like for *your* team. They also can't help you assess for specialized skills like reading X-rays or writing code.

At the end of the day, *you* are the person who ultimately owns the team you build. Successful hiring managers form close partnerships with the recruiting team to identify, interview, and close the best people. A great recruiter brings her network as well as her knowledge of the recruiting process—how to source and pitch candidates, how to guide them through interviews, and how to negotiate offers. A great hiring manager brings her understanding of the role—what it needs and why it's exciting—as well as her time to personally connect with candidates.

If you aren't working with a recruiter, then you'll need to play both roles yourself. Here's how you should approach working together.

Describe Your Ideal Candidate as Precisely as You Can

It's the hiring manager's job to identify when a role is open and what kinds of people would be the best fit. Write the job description yourself and be specific about the skills or experiences you are looking for.

Even within the same kind of job, the specific requirements can vary meaningfully from team to team. For example, some of the designers on my team are responsible for our most widely used features, such as browsing posts or commenting. The candidates they look for are extremely detail oriented, with strong craftsmanship skills. Others on my team work on designing experiences for specific audiences, whether they are small-business owners, gamers, or new internet users. These teams seek designers who are empathetic and experienced with research methodologies to guide their work. When your recruiter understands those nuances, he can help you screen for people who have the qualities you're looking for.

Develop a Sourcing Strategy

Once you have a good sense of the kind of person you want, it's helpful to sit down with the recruiter and brainstorm where to look for your ideal candidate. You might come up with specific titles or organizations to search for on LinkedIn, people whom you can ping for recommendations, conferences to attend, or ads you'd like to place.

Another exercise is to figure out which patterns or keywords you should look for in a résumé. For one role, my recruiting partner and I identified that our ideal candidate would have experience working at both a design agency as well as a tech company because that combination often produces a healthy balance of vision and pragmatic know-how. We also agreed that I should send out the introductory email instead of the recruiter so the experience felt personal right off the bat.

Sometimes, unusual patterns can lead to amazing candidates. Patty McCord, the former chief talent officer at Netflix, describes how her recruiting team noticed that a surprising number of their top data-science leaders shared an interest in music. So in addition to searching for résumés with the typical data-oriented keywords, they also began looking for people who played piano or guitar. "[We] concluded that such people can easily toggle between their left and right brains—a great skill for data analysis," McCord writes.

Deliver an Amazing Interview Experience

I can't tell you how many times I have had candidates accept and tell me that part of their reason for doing so was because the interview process felt so attentive, focused, and fast. It gave them confidence in our company and the team they would be working with.

Even when you don't end up extending an offer, an amazing interview experience tells prospective hires that you care about the people who might be the future of your organization.

Making this happen requires a strong manager–recruiter relationship. My recruiting partner and I become like Batman and Robin for any candidate who comes in to interview. We'd message each other multiple times a day about the details—did all the interviewers have the background notes? Who was assessing which skills? Could we find an interviewer who'd relate well to the candidate, like Anne, who came from the same previous company, or Dixon, who was also new to the city? Who was going to reach out and thank the candidate for his time?

By working in tandem on the interview experience, we avoided common mistakes like leaving days or weeks in between next steps, asking candidates to repeat themselves over and over, or giving them conflicting or confusing information.

Show Candidates How Much You Want Them

When you decide to extend an offer, it's as much your job as it is the recruiter's to make the candidate feel that you want her to say yes. The more distance you create in the process—for example, letting a week lapse between communications—the more likely the answer is no.

After I deliver an offer, I try to check in with the candidate every other day to let her know that I am thinking about her and that I'm excited to welcome her to my team. I ask if she'd like to talk through any questions, and sometimes we'll do lunch or dinner to discuss the role in more detail.

The more senior the candidate, the more critical your involvement is in the close because that person likely has many options, and you are looking for her to play a leadership role within your team. Paint a vivid picture of how you see her having impact. Help her understand why the role is exciting and why she's the perfect person to tackle these big problems.

HIRING IS A GAMBLE, BUT MAKE SMART BETS

How likely is it that a few hours spent with someone will give you an accurate sense of their potential as an employee?

We might think we are good judges of character, but the evidence suggests otherwise. A few years ago, Google crunched the numbers on tens of thousands of interviews to see if there was a correlation between how high an interviewer rated the interaction and how well the candidate went on to perform. What they found was that there was "zero relationship" and that it was "a complete random mess."

I wasn't surprised to read this because I've seen examples on both sides—where an amazing interview led us to hiring someone who ultimately wasn't a good fit, and when I said, "No hire," to someone who turned out to be an incredible contributor.

There are three reasons why a handful of interviews isn't ever going to be a perfectly reliable predictor of someone's success. The first is that it's impossible to re-create the actual working environment of a team in a thirty-minute or hour-long meeting. Most real-world projects are complex, spanning many people and taking weeks, months, or years to complete. An interview can only hope to simulate how well a candidate does on a smaller problem in a fraction of the time.

Second, interviewers bring their personal biases into the evaluation. We're swayed by first impressions and whether what we see fits our understanding of what a "great" candidate looks like. A Harvard study found that when American symphonies implemented "blind auditions"—that is, the interviewers listened to a candidate play from behind a curtain—it improved the probability that a woman would advance from preliminary rounds by 50 percent.

Finally, the third reason interview results don't tell the whole truth is that people are capable of enormous change. Google stopped relying on signals like college GPAs for candidates more than a few years out of school. Said Laszlo Bock, their senior vice president of people operations, "After two or three years, your ability to perform at Google is completely unrelated to how you performed when you were in school because the skills you required in college are very different. You're also fundamentally a different person. You learn and grow, you think about things differently."

Hiring someone new is always risky, but be smart about your approach and you'll raise your chances of success.

Examine Past Examples of Similar Work

The best—though still imperfect—predictor for how someone will do in the future is to understand how they've done in the past on similar projects in similar environments. That's why internships are so valuable; when someone joins your team for a few months, you get a much better understanding of how they work.

The next best thing is to dive deeply into their past work. When we interview designers, we put a strong emphasis on the "portfolio review," where candidates come in and present a few projects of their choosing. By hearing them talk through their process and show us specific examples of their work, we learn a lot about their skills and their approach to problems. A friend who works in education does something similar by asking potential instructors to come in and teach a class on whatever subject they'd like.

Ask candidates if they can show you the applications they've developed, the articles they've written, the pitches they've given, etc., so you can assess the quality of their output. If what's presented is a team effort, ask for clarification on which pieces the individual was responsible for.

Seek Out Trusted Recommendations

If a credible source tells you that Jane is amazing but Jack is not someone he'd want to work with again, take that feedback seriously. The trustworthiness of your two-hour interview pales in comparison to the testimony of someone's tried-and-true experience working with that person.

Whenever we open up a new role, the first thing I do is make sure my entire team knows we're hiring. "If you could wave a magic wand, who's your dream candidate for this position?" I'll ask them. The list I get in return is both a good starting point on who I should reach out to, but also where else we could be sourcing from—across these recommended people, are there patterns in skills, companies, or experiences that we should further dig in to?

The other place where trusted recommendations come in handy is the reference check. Kevin Ryan, founder of Gilt Groupe and *Business Insider*, takes personal references to the extreme. "The hiring process typically has three elements: the résumé, the interview, and the reference check," says Ryan. "Most managers overvalue the résumé and interview and undervalue the reference check. References matter most."

The key, Ryan says, is to look for honest references. "It can take real effort to find someone who'll be straight with you, but it's worth it." You probably won't get that by calling up the folks that a candidate provides or talking to someone you don't know well. But ask your network of trusted colleagues if they can help put you in touch with a mutual connection that they also trust.

When evaluating references, keep in mind two things. The first is that people typically improve their skills over time, so discount negative feedback that isn't recent. If your friend tells you that five years ago Jack wasn't great at closing deals, it's possible he's since gotten much better.

The second thing is that you might not get a diverse pool of candidates if you're *only* sourcing within your existing network, so go back to your definition of the ideal person for the role and make sure you're casting the net wide enough.

Get Multiple Interviewers Involved

The best practice for interviews is to have the candidate talk to multiple people who know what the role needs, with each interviewer asking different questions so that the group emerges with a well-rounded perspective. For example, if you are hiring a finance manager, one interviewer might assess management and collaboration skills while another asks detailed finance questions, and yet another explores the candidate's past work experience.

Having multiple interviewers can reduce bias and catch subtle red flags that any one person might have missed. When debriefing, however, each person should independently record their rationale and their final "hire" or "no hire" decision before hearing other interviewers' thoughts to ensure that the discussion doesn't lead to groupthink.

Look for Passionate Advocates Rather Than Consensus

When we started ramping up the number of interviews we did, one of the things I started to hear in debriefs was what we called the "weak hire." The weak hire was when all the interviewers independently landed on the side of "hire," which sounds great on paper—a unanimous decision!—but nobody was particularly enthusiastic about it. This manifested in phrases like, "I'm not sure he'd be right for *my* team, but I could see him being valuable on someone else's team" or "I don't see a reason why we *shouldn't* hire her . . ."

I noticed that weak hires were given when a candidate didn't have any obvious issues—they seemed pleasant enough, they toed the standard line in their answers, and they had relevant experience. At the same time, they also didn't *wow* in any particular dimension. None of the interviewers felt strongly enough to fight for the hire if the decision came down to no.

Since every hire is already a gamble, reject any weak hires. While they're not likely to bomb, they're also not likely to add much. If you're going to make a bet, bet on someone with a passionate advocate behind her. If a candidate gets mixed reviews but all the interviewers that said hire are adamant about wanting to work with her, it's usually a sign that she brings something highly valued to the table.

Prepare Your Interview Questions Ahead of Time

The best interviews happen when you show up with a clear sense of what you want to learn about the person. This means that you should familiarize yourself with their background and have a list of questions prepared. If multiple candidates are interviewing for the same role, ask each candidate the same things. Remember that we are all biased—if you don't do this, you risk basing your hiring decision on your impression of the person and the flow of the conversation rather than on the substance of his answers.

I once interviewed a candidate, let's call him Mason, who came off nervous and timid. Mason didn't make much eye contact, took breathy gasps in between sentences, and would repeat the same point three times in an answer. But I had prepared a set of questions to understand his skills and experience: Could he walk me through how he set goals on a particular project? Could he describe the most difficult challenge he'd encountered in his past job and how he tackled it? Could he honestly describe his strengths and weaknesses (and did he admit that one of those weaknesses was communication)?

These questions helped me understand how Mason handled problems, and he nailed them. The substance of his answers were more detailed and thoughtful than other candidates'. We hired him. He worked hard to improve his communication skills, and he quickly became a top contributor.

Only you can decide what questions you should ask, because only you know what you're looking for. In particular, highly specialized roles deserve specific questions that probe at those skills. But if you're looking for a starting point on what to ask, these are my favorite all-purpose questions:

1. *What kinds of challenges are interesting to you and why? Can you describe a favorite project?* This tells me what a candidate is passionate about.

2. *What do you consider your greatest strengths? What would your peers agree are your areas of growth?* This question gets both at a candidate's self-awareness and what his actual strengths and weaknesses might be.

3. *Imagine yourself in three years. What do you hope will be different about you then compared to now?* This lets me understand the candidate's ambitions as well as how goal oriented and self-reflective she is.

4. *What was the hardest conflict you've had in the past year? How did it end, and what did you learn from the experience?* This gives me a sense of how the candidate works with other people and how he approaches conflict.

5. *What's something that's inspired you in your work recently?* This sheds light on what the candidate thinks is interesting or valuable.

Reject Anyone Who Exhibits Toxic Behavior

Remember how assholes are the one thing you shouldn't tolerate on your team? Be on the lookout for warning signs in interviews: bad-mouthing past employers ("My last manager was terrible"); blaming failures they were associated with on others ("The reason my last project didn't succeed was because of internal politics"); insulting other groups of people ("The sales team were bozos"); asking what the company can do for them instead of the reverse ("This feels like a step up for my career"); and coming across with high arrogance or low self-awareness ("I was attracted to this position because it seems like you need someone really senior").

Build a Team with Diverse Perspectives

A long time ago, as our team was growing, my manager Kate started the process of hiring for some new leadership roles. I remember sitting through presentation after presentation by external candidates from big-name companies. They'd walk us through polished decks explaining their elaborate design processes: creating intricate user personas, conducting months-long research, hosting idea-generation sprints involving hundreds of Post-it notes.

At the time, Facebook was still small, and I had a hard time understanding why you wouldn't just get into a room with some engineers to build and design a product in a few weeks. These fancy processes seemed like overhead. Would big-company veterans work out in our scrappy start-up environment? I wasn't convinced. But after Kate made a few hires, I got my answer.

At first, I found myself clashing with the new managers—we disagreed on hiring strategy, how to run a critique, what an A-plus designer looked like, and more. To be honest, I thought the "new guard" was trying to make things more complicated, and they thought I was being closed-minded.

But time always reveals the truth. It turns out that as we grew, having managers in our midst who knew what to do when we went from 50 to 250 people was a tremendous asset. Bit by bit, I started to appreciate that their strengths were my weaknesses. We indeed had to evolve how we worked, including hiring for new types of talent, introducing more structured processes, and, yes, better supporting our growing user base by adopting tools like personas and sprints.

Prioritizing diversity isn't just a poster or a slogan. It's the belief that diversity in all aspects—from gender to race to work history to life experiences—leads to better ideas and better results. The science supports this: A 2014 report of hundreds of public companies found that those with the greatest ethnic and racial diversity in their management ranks were 35 percent more likely to have financial returns higher than average. A study of 2,400 companies found that organizations with at least one female board member had better outcomes than organizations with no women. An experiment involving college fraternities and sororities found that teams consisting of an "outsider" solved problems more accurately than teams consisting just of people within the group.

Even if you don't look at the data, it just makes logical sense: Are you more likely to get innovative ideas from a bunch of other people who look, think, and behave like you, or from people who come with different perspectives?

Prioritizing diversity means that you actively seek out candidates who offer something different. It means not just promoting from within but also hiring from the outside. And it means recognizing that every single person, you and me included, comes with his or her own bag of beliefs that should be challenged by others. The power of diversity helps our team avoid biases, make better decisions, and think more creatively.

Hire People Who Are Capable of More

Sometimes, I'll hear managers say things like: "I only need someone to take care of X right now. I don't need someone who can also do Y and Z."

Maybe. You certainly shouldn't look at CEO candidates when the role (and the budget) calls for a frontline salesperson. At the same time, if you're dealing with knowledge work, hiring someone who seems to offer more than what the role needs right now means they can help you tackle bigger problems in the future. In all my years of building teams, I have never, ever thought to myself, *huh, there aren't enough big problems for all the talented people we have.*

The opposite has always been true. I once hired a director-level candidate when we were starting up a new initiative. The initial size of the team was modest, and this hire had experience running much larger organizations. On paper, the role seemed too small for what he was capable of.

But fast-forward to a few months later: he's killing it on the area he's asked to lead, and he proactively identifies and executes on other initiatives that help us scale. When an opportunity to lead another team comes up, he's the first person I think of. Within a year, he's managing multiple key projects.

As a manager, one of the smartest ways to multiply your team's impact is to hire the best people and empower them to do more and more until you stretch the limits of their capabilities.

Meeting Frogs Is Part of the Deal, but Believe in the Process

For me, the most stressful part of hiring was the uncertainty of it. If I emailed a candidate, there was no guarantee that I would hear back. If I got a response and we set up a phone call, there was a good chance that either the candidate or I would decide afterward that the role wasn't a good match.

In the cases where the candidate came in to interview, he or she might not do well on our questions. And if we *finally* made it to the end with a shining offer ready to be signed, the candidate would sometimes decline. At every step, you could be met with disappointment and a sense that you had wasted your time.

The thing I learned, though, is that if you zoom out a little further, the recruiting progress can be simply understood as a funnel of numbers. When you are talking about dozens of candidates, that funnel stays relatively consistent. For example (and I am making up the numbers here), out of twenty emails you send, you might get interest back from ten. Out of ten initial meetings, four will move on to interview stage. Out of four interviews, one will result in an offer. And out of an offer, a candidate will decline 50 percent of the time.

Though the specific numbers might be different given the team, the role, and the organization, no matter what you plug in, it's possible to get to an equation that looks like this: "An average of X initial emails leads to a hire."

Thinking about things this way made me confident that the more time and energy I spend on recruiting, the more it pays off, even if a few specific instances here and there don't work out.

HIRING WHEN YOU NEED FIVE, TEN, OR HUNDREDS OF PEOPLE

A few years back, our company was growing rapidly, and design hiring had not kept pace. It seemed like every single day, I heard another tale of woe about how our shortage of designers was creating problems—projects were stalled, the existing designers felt stretched thin, frustrations abounded. "But I'm working on it!" I'd cry in response. And I was. There wasn't a day that went by where I wasn't messaging with the recruiting team, sending out cold emails, or conducting interviews. "I want to hire great people," I'd say. "And hiring well takes time."

A few weeks after that, my manager Chris and I were having our usual 1:1, when the topic turned to my open positions. "Do you think you're spending enough time on hiring?" he asked me. "Yes," I said, and gave him my standard line about how I never let a day pass without working on recruiting. There was a long pause. Then, he looked me in the eye and asked: "If I told you that hiring well was the *only* thing that mattered, would you do anything differently?"

I blinked. Well, when he put it *that* way, yes, of course. I was working on hiring every day, but the majority of my time was spent on other things—reviewing road maps, critiquing designs, meeting with my reports, etc. When I looked at hiring as the *only* thing I needed to excel at, suddenly dozens of new ideas zoomed forth. I could be asking my network for more referrals. I could be inviting more candidates out for coffee. I could be honing my pitch with trusted colleagues.

The four months that followed were the most productive I'd ever been. I filled all my open leadership roles, and we welcomed many new talented faces onto our staff.

What I learned is that hiring is not dissimilar to tackling a design problem. When you start, you don't know what the answer is or how long it will take. But you trust in the process. If you put in the time and energy—if you come up with ten different design options, say, or if you talk to ten candidates—eventually you will find the best solution. You always do.

We've already established that recruiting is a critical part of any manager's job. However, when your team is growing swiftly, hiring becomes easily the top one or two most important skills. If you need to build out a large team and you don't have a strong bench of managers, the problem quickly becomes intractable. You can't create great outcomes without consistently attracting talented people and ensuring that they can also hire well.

Here are the most important things I've learned about hiring at scale.

Successful Hiring Is All about Diligent Execution

Depending on your luck, it might take you two weeks or two months to land someone for a particular role. However, at scale, when you need to grow by twenty or two hundred people instead of just two, the averages start to massage away individual cases of unpredictability. If, for your team, one accept comes from two offers, eight interviews, twenty initial meetings, and forty emails, then to get twenty hires, you'll need to send about 800 emails over the course of the year. It's a big number, but the certainty is refreshing.

Your task then becomes to create a well-oiled machine in which all the steps in the recruiting funnel happen smoothly and efficiently. Let's say there are eight managers on your team. To reach your hiring goals, each manager will need to send out roughly two hundred emails a year, which is about four a week. That's not too crazy. If you want to achieve 160 interviews, you should aim to have three candidates come in every week. You'll need to have enough people who can assess candidates in a consistent and objective manner, which means you'll need a program to train interviewers.

Look also for opportunities to make your funnel more efficient. Can you tweak your initial email to be more compelling so that you get more responses? Can you host events so that prospective candidates are more likely to want to interview? Can you come up with better questions to ask that give you more information about a candidate?

Your success depends on how well you operate. Break the problem down into smaller and smaller pieces, and ask your entire staff to play a role in helping the team grow and thrive.

Do Your Research When Hiring Leaders

Hiring a manager or senior contributor onto your team is a big investment, and bad leadership hires are disproportionately more disruptive because they affect more people. If you bring on a new manager whose values aren't aligned with yours, he will hire people that you may not think are a good fit. If he turns out to be a crummy collaborator, you'll be dealing with a line of complaints out the door.

It's wise not to rush into leadership hires, and instead make sure you know what an ideal applicant looks like. The easiest way to do that is to talk with as many prospective candidates as you can, including those who may not want the job but know the role well. Especially if you're hiring for an unfamiliar position, you need to do your homework to understand what the bar should be.

Imagine a smart CEO with a background in sales trying to find a head of engineering. She's never done the job before, so how will she know what to look for? She could start by asking her network to connect her with top engineering leaders. Even if they're not interested in her position, she invites them out for coffee so she can learn from them: What do they look for in a résumé? What questions do they ask in interviews, and what kinds of answers are they looking for? Do they have any recommendations on where to look for strong candidates?

Our CEO then talks with the engineers on her team to understand what they think is important in a leader. She asks a few of them to help her assess a candidate's technical skills. She makes sure to bring in a variety of people to interview so she can become better calibrated on what to look for. As a result, she makes confident hiring decisions and brings in a top-notch engineering leader.

When you make a great leadership hire, the impact on your team is enormous for years to come. Don't approach it willy-nilly—it pays to do your research.

Take the Long View with Top Talent

This happens so often that it's practically a cliché: I'm actively recruiting for an amazing leader. I meet someone who impresses me, and immediately, my eyes get starry with the possibilities. I envision us tackling problems together and having a blast. I'm already thinking about how I'll introduce this person to the team on her first day.

Excitedly, I give her the offer, and everything is coming up roses until . . . I get the dreaded phone call: "Actually, I've decided to do something else. . . ." Crushed, I wish her well and slump back into my chair. I cross her name off the list. The search continues.

But, see, this story has a happy ending. Because months or

years down the road, I get an email out of the blue. It's from the candidate. The situation has changed, she says, and now she's ready for something new. Are there any opportunities on my team?

The lesson: Recruiting top talent is all about the relationships you build. Good, seasoned leaders aren't short of options, because everybody wants to hire them. When they're looking for their next role, they tend to choose opportunities that they already know to be great. Maybe a good friend works at and loves Company Y. Or maybe they've met some of the leaders of Company X before. If you could get a job anywhere, why would you join a team where you don't know a soul?

That's why attracting the best people is a long-term investment. Pay attention to the rising stars of your field and get to know them through conferences, mixers, and other events. Continuously build your network. And develop your team's reputation as well, whether through participating in the community, contributing new learnings to your field, telling your story in the press, or simply through being known as a class act.

Even with the many, many declined offers I've gotten over the years, I've come to realize that they weren't for nothing. Many of the leaders on my team today only joined after saying no once or twice before. Nowadays, I tell people who turn us down that I hope our paths cross again. Jobs may be short, but careers are long. Perhaps we didn't have the right opportunity at the right moment or they weren't ready to do something new yet. One day that could change, and when it does, I want them to think of us.

Build a Great Bench

One of the scenarios I play out with the leaders on my team is what I call the "extended vacation" test. (Others have used the term "hit by the bus," but that's just morbid.) It goes like this: If you were to hike some distant mountains or sunbathe on a remote island for a few months, how much would your own manager need to step in to ensure that everything ran smoothly?

If the answer is "not much," then congratulations! You've got a great bench. If the answer is, "Hmm, my manager would need to do a lot," then that's a sign your next layer of leadership could use some shoring up.

Having a great bench means your lieutenants could take over for you if you're unexpectedly called out of the office. It means you are not the single point of failure—fires won't ignite, chaos won't erupt, and work won't grind to a halt if you're not there. Having a great bench is one of the strongest signs of stellar leadership because it means the team you've built can steer the ship and thrive, even if you are not at the helm.

"But wait," I hear people say. "That sounds nice in theory, but if your team can be successful without you, doesn't that mean you're not actually valuable?"

Excellent question. But ask yourself: Can even the best leaders be coached to even better performance? The answer is absolutely yes, so you should still see your job as being a multiplier for your people.

More important, a strong bench frees up a manager to tackle the next big hill on the horizon. When Facebook was still run out of a Harvard dorm room, Mark Zuckerberg personally wrote most of the code for the service. Hiring his first engineers didn't mean that he became obsolete; it just meant that he could focus his attention on other things—expanding the service to other schools, developing new features like News Feed, and hiring other leaders to work with him on the goal of connecting the world.

The job your team does shouldn't be static—as the group becomes capable of more, your ambitions should also grow. What is the next big problem that your team can take on, and how can you help make it happen?

Facebook today would be fine if Mark went on an extended

vacation—in fact, he took a few months off after the births of his daughters. But his leadership continues to challenge the company to dream bigger and do more in the service of bringing people closer together.

Create a Culture That Prioritizes Hiring Well

If your team is growing to the point of needing more managers, the responsibility of hiring must become shared. Eventually, you won't be in every interview, nor be the deciding vote in every debrief. That simply isn't sustainable at tens or hundreds of hires a year.

On the one hand, you might feel like you're losing control, like you're "giving away your LEGOs," as my friend Molly Graham calls it. Molly is well acquainted with hyper-growth through her time at Google, Facebook, and other start-ups. She likens the anxiety you might feel to that of a kid who was once the solo architect and now has to share her building blocks with others.

On the other hand, you have the chance to establish a culture that outlasts you and carries forth your values at a broader scale. To do this, pay close attention to how you set the tone for hiring. Coach your leaders to treat team building with the utmost care, and ensure that they dedicate enough time and attention to connecting with remarkable candidates. Repeatedly talk about your values so that everyone understands what great talent looks like. And, above all, make it clear that building the team isn't just one person's job, it's everyone's job.

During our monthly design meetings, one long-standing tradition we have is going around the room and introducing any new employees in our midst. At first, it felt like I was hosting a dinner party where I'd present one of my new acquaintances to some old friends of mine. Over time, other managers began introducing the hires they made.

One day, as we did this ritual with a giant room full of people, I glanced around at all the new faces and realized that I didn't know a single one of them! It was a surprising realization, but also one of my proudest moments. As we went from person to person, it was clear that these new hires were amazing. I didn't hire them directly myself, but I couldn't wait to work with them.

Chapter Eight

Making Things Happen

AVOID

ASPIRE

Once upon a time, a guy named Kevin who loved Kentucky whiskey wanted to create something that helped people make plans with their friends, check into different locations, and post photos of the gatherings. He quickly hacked together an app called Burbn and launched it into the world. He persuaded his friend Mike to join him, and together they carefully observed how people used their app.

It turns out that what they built was complicated and not particularly useful. Users weren't checking in much, which was the main point of the service. But there was one feature that seemed to be sticking—the photo-sharing part. People were posting snaps of everyday life—streets and restaurants, lattes and beers, friends and selfies. Fascinated, Kevin and Mike dug in to this use case. They studied all the ways people shared photos using their phones. A few months later, they decided to pivot their app. They cut out the planning and location check-in features and made the focus all about simple, beautiful photo sharing. Oh, and they changed the name, too, from Burbn to Instagram.

Today, Instagram is used by more than 1 billion people all over the world. In 2012, it became part of the Facebook family after a $1 billion acquisition.

The origin story of every great company reveals a common theme: The path to success is never a straight line. It's not about having the single, brilliant, lightning-flash insight that suddenly wins the game. Instead, it's about consistent planning and execution—

you try what seems like a good idea. You do it quickly. You keep your mind open and curious. You learn. Then you scrap what failed and double down on what's working. You rinse and repeat, maybe over and over and over again. This process is what makes things happen.

Process. Many people think of it as a bad word because it conjures up images of filling out paperwork or waiting in line. But process isn't inherently good or bad. Process is simply the answer to the question "What actions do we take to achieve our goals?" Even if that answer isn't written down anywhere, it still exists.

Bad process is heavy and arbitrary. It feels like a series of hoops to jump through. But good process is what helps us execute at our best. We learn from our mistakes, move quickly, and make smarter decisions for the future.

How can you establish effective processes for your team? This chapter discusses some of the fundamentals of making things happen.

START WITH A CONCRETE VISION

Once, I was working on a six-month road map for our Groups product. I wanted to start by stating the purpose behind our work, so I wrote down: *Help people connect with others through their shared interests.* Then I went on to describe our strategy and upcoming milestones.

At my next 1:1 with my manager Chris, I shared the document with him to get some feedback. He read the first sentence, took out a pen, and underlined: *Help people connect with others through their shared interests.* "It's too soft," he muttered. "What do you mean?" I asked. It seemed to me a perfectly accurate description of what we were trying to do. He tried again: "It's just—you know, it's squishy. It doesn't actually describe what's going to be different."

I got his point then. Though it's common to hear words like

help, *improve*, or *enhance* when talking about goals, they don't paint a clear picture. If someone on the team fixes one bug, does that "improve" the experience? Of course. Does it contribute to *helping people connect with others through their shared interests*? Sure. But would our team be happy if that's all we did in the next six months? No way. Because of the huge amount of subjectivity in words like *help* or *improve*, they don't do much to create a shared sense of purpose.

Instead, tangible visions have the most impact. Recall Herbert Hoover's catchy campaign slogan: "A chicken in every pot." It's the opposite of squishy. The promise isn't "America's going to get wealthier." It's not "People will have more economic prosperity." "A chicken in every pot" conjures up an image of millions of families enjoying a hearty and substantial meal for supper.

It turns out that Herbert Hoover never said this. The phrase comes from a Republican campaign flyer posted around the time of the election. But the memorability of that little promise spread far and wide, into nearly a century of misattribution. That's the power of a concrete vision.

When Facebook was a little-known site used by millions of students, Mark Zuckerberg would casually say that, one day, we'd connect the entire world. At the time, MySpace was almost ten times bigger than us, so this felt like outlandish ambition. And yet. The vision was razor sharp. Nobody could misunderstand what we were going after. We weren't just trying to "grow and improve the service." We weren't even aiming to be the number one player in social networking. We held the idea in our minds that, one day, we'd build something useful enough that *everyone*—all the billions of people out there—would use it.

An inspiring vision is bold. It doesn't hedge. You know instantly whether you've hit it or not because it's measurable. And it's easily repeated, from one person to the next to the next. It doesn't describe the *how*—your team will figure that out—it simply describes what the outcome will be. I tell my team that I'll know they did a good job describing their vision if I randomly ask five people who've heard it to repeat it to me and they all say the exact same thing.

As a manager, it's important to define and share a concrete vision for your team that describes what you're collectively trying to achieve. An SAT tutoring service might state its objective as improving every student's test scores by at least two hundred points. A lab might commit to having a 50 percent reduction in error rates within two years. The fund-raising arm of a nonprofit may set a goal to raise $50 million in three years. For Groups, our mission eventually became to enable one billion people to find a meaningful community on Facebook.

To help you get started, ask yourself the following:

- Assume you have a magic wand that makes everything your team does go perfectly. What do you hope will be different in two to three years compared to now?

- How would you want someone who works on an adjacent team to describe what your team does? What do you hope will be your team's reputation in a few years? How far off is that from where things are today?

- What unique superpower(s) does your team have? When you're at your best, how are you creating value? What would it look like for your team to be twice as good? Five times as good?

- If you had to create a quick litmus test that anyone could use to assess whether your team was doing a poor job, a mediocre job, or a kick-ass job, what would that litmus test be?

Create a Believable Game Plan

Let's say you have a concrete vision and you know what success looks like. What then? Now you have to figure out a plan—also known as creating a strategy—to make those outcomes real.

"Plans are worthless, but planning is everything," said Dwight D. Eisenhower, one of history's top generals and the orchestrator of D-day during World War II. Though surprises happen and not everything is within our control, it's through the process of planning that we make sense of our situation and plot our best shot at success. When emergencies do arise, a solid strategy provides the foundation for us to quickly adapt our plans instead of going back to the chaos of square one.

What makes for a good strategy? First, it must have a realistic shot at working. If someone asks you what your strategy is for getting "a lemonade stand on every block" and you say that you're going to get all the top celebrities in the world to endorse it, you'll be met with raised eyebrows. Doing so will require either so much money that it's unlikely to be a good investment, or a product that's so amazing that the LeBron Jameses and Taylor Swifts of the world *want* to be associated with it even if you don't pay them—also improbable.

A good strategy understands the crux of the problem it's trying to solve. It focuses a team's unique strengths, resources, and energy on what matters the most in achieving its goals.

If you're leading a smaller part of a larger organization, then your team's plans should relate directly to the organization's top-level strategy. For example, Facebook seeks to give people the power to build community and bring the world closer together through tools like News Feed, Messenger, and Groups. Within those product teams, the leaders are tasked with creating the specific strategies for their area to support Facebook's mission.

As you plan for the future, here are some things to keep in mind.

Craft a Plan Based on Your Team's Strengths

Just as your management style reflects who you are and what you're good at, so too should your plans take into account your team's unique capabilities. For example, my team of product designers are experts at mobile and desktop interaction design. These are the skills that we hire and train for because it's the bulk of what we do. But in those instances when a project calls for a polished marketing video or a large number of illustrations, I usually turn to another team.

Sometimes, this confuses my engineering colleagues. "But aren't you designers?" they ask. "Designers draw and animate, right?" I explain that while many people on our team *can*, that doesn't mean we *should*. It's not our core competency, and we'll probably end up spending double the time for 80 percent the quality of what a specialized team could do.

Just like you wouldn't send an army's cavalry on a spying mission, you shouldn't create a plan that doesn't match what your team is well suited for. There are usually dozens of ways to get from Point A to Point B. Do you want to go by land, sea, or air? If you choose land, do you want to take the jungle path or the mountain path? There is no universal right answer. The plan that is smartest for your team is the one that acknowledges your relative strengths and weaknesses.

Focus on Doing a Few Things Well

Ever heard of the Pareto principle? Named after an Italian economist who observed an interesting pattern of wealth distribution in nineteenth-century Italy, it's now more commonly known as the 80/20 principle thanks to a blockbuster book by Richard Koch written in 1998. The general idea is that the majority of the results come from a minority of the causes. The key is identifying which things matter the most.

Conventional wisdom says that success comes from working hard and persevering through difficulties. That's sage advice, but it overlooks how important focus is. As Koch writes, "Few people take objectives really seriously. They put average effort into too many things, rather than superior thought and effort into a few important things. People who achieve the most are selective as well as determined."

When creating new products, builders must determine which features are essential and which are "nice to have." When forming a new team, managers try to hire the leaders or "anchors" before the rest of the group. When determining which patients to see in the emergency room, doctors will triage and tackle the most urgent issues first. Prioritization is key, and it's an essential managerial skill.

The best way to practice prioritization is to order any list you make by importance. Make sure that the things at the top are taken care of before you venture further down the list. For example, if you've got five tasks on your to-do list for today, rank them by priority and do number one before number two. If you have three goals for your team this half, force yourself to answer: "If I could only achieve one goal, which would it be?" If you have five open roles to hire for, pour your energy into filling the one that's most critical.

Effort doesn't count; results are what matter. I learned this my first week on the job when I was told the origin story of one of Facebook's most popular products. In 2005, Facebook launched a way for people to upload personal photos onto the service. At the time, there were many other photo-sharing options to choose from. Among them, Flickr was the gold standard. It was chock-full of features—high-resolution photos beautifully displayed (including a full-screen slideshow mode), photo search by location or even color, slick navigation with previews and keyboard shortcuts, and much more.

By contrast, Facebook's initial product seemed incredibly bare-bones. You could only upload low-resolution photos, so they showed up small and grainy. There were no handy navigation shortcuts, no search capabilities, no full-screen displays. Flickr had a much bigger team that had been working on these features for years, whereas Facebook's photo service was built by a handful of engineers in a matter of months. But there was one small, novel feature that the team included in their initial launch: photo tagging. The idea was that you could indicate that a particular photo was of you and your friend Susan, and Susan would get notified about it. The tagged photo would then also show up on Susan's profile so that other mutual friends could see it.

This photo-tagging feature was so powerful that, within a few short years, Facebook became the most popular photo-sharing service in the world. Why? Because it turns out that the most valued part of personal photos are the people within them. In most homes, what you see hung on the walls or lining the mantels aren't snapshots of beautiful landscapes or artsy scenes but rather *faces*—family portraits, weddings and graduations, memories of happy afternoons spent with loved ones. The tagging functionality ensured that those in the photos, as well as their friends, would not miss seeing them. This simple social feature was worth way more to people than dozens of other less useful features.

In the words of Apple visionary Steve Jobs, creator of the iPod, iPhone, and iPad: "People think focus means saying yes to the thing you've got to focus on. But that's not what it means at all. It means saying no to the hundred other good ideas that there are. You have to pick carefully. I'm actually as proud of the things we haven't done as the things I have done. Innovation is saying no to 1,000 things."

Define Who Is Responsible for What

Imagine this scenario: Five people are brainstorming ways to improve the ease of moving through an app. The ideas come fast and furious, ricocheting off the walls and stirring up debate.

"We should allow swiping between sections!" someone exclaims. "But is swiping something that people will discover?" someone else asks. "Let's do some research to understand that," comes the answer. "Good idea. We can also talk to Jane, whose team tried a similar thing a year ago, and ask what they learned." "I'm not sure about swiping—could be good, but what do you think about floating tabs?" someone else pipes up. And on and on the conversation goes.

Based on that, what do you expect are the next steps around swiping?

The most likely answer is that nothing happens. While there was talk of doing some research and talking to Jane, no action item was created because no one explicitly signed up to do it. When ownership isn't clear, things slip through the cracks. This doesn't just happen in meetings; every time you send an email to more than one person about an issue that requires a follow-up, the recipients may be confused about whom you are expecting to do what. Each might assume someone else is responsible.

I'm embarrassed to admit how long it took me to realize the importance of defining ownership. Even when people have the best of intentions, fuzziness around role definition can create problems. One time, I sat two of my most talented team members down and told them about a challenging new problem. I asked them to work together to come up with a solution. In my head, I thought that their strengths would complement each other well.

The problem was that they had widely differing opinions about what to do. Because I didn't define how I wanted them to work together or who ultimately had decision-making authority, they argued in circles, each trying to convince the other. Progress slowed to a halt. From this, I learned that the clearer I am about whom I'm holding accountable for what, the less of a chance there is for ambiguity and crossed wires.

In retrospect, here's how I should have clarified expectations up front: "Dan, I'd like you to take the lead on framing the options; Sarah, can you own defining the visual language?" or "Each of you should take a stab at how you'd design this. For the areas where you have differing opinions, let's have the three of us get together and I'll make a call."

Break Down a Big Goal into Smaller Pieces

Have you ever heard of Parkinson's law? Coined by Cyril Parkinson, a twentieth-century British historian and scholar, it states: "Work expands so as to fill the time available for its completion."

When my publishing team and I first started discussing the schedule for this book, we agreed that a sensible timeline for a first draft was one year. I got off the phone call feeling bold. *One year is* more *than enough time. I'll have the first draft done in six months*, I told myself.

Guess what? I sent off a not-even-fully-completed first draft on the one-year mark, feeling abashed. For the first nine months, I felt as though there was plenty of time on the clock. So if another urgent task came up, or if I simply didn't feel like writing, I'd tell myself, *Skipping one day won't make much of a difference*.

For my second draft, I wised up. Instead of treating the entire book as one humongous project with a far-out deadline, I broke it down and promised my editors I would revise one chapter a week.

Suddenly, I became far more disciplined. If I wanted to hit my goal, I had to edit about two pages a night. Translated into these smaller milestones, it was easy to see that missing even a night's worth of writing was a big deal because I'd have to make up for it to stay on track. I made good on my word—my efficiency tripled on the second draft.

Nothing worthwhile happens overnight. Every big dream is the culmination of thousands of tiny steps forward. When Facebook first launched, the only thing you could do was fill out a profile, and the only place it worked was at Harvard University. Week over week, Mark and the founders focused on expanding the service one school at a time, one feature at a time.

Thinking only about the finish line of a long race can be discouraging because it seems miles and miles away. You might wonder if anything you do today can really make a difference. But if you divide your plan up into smaller chunks and focus on your next milestone—finishing the task at hand, preparing for that next meeting, getting through two pages—success suddenly seems entirely within your reach. And the sense of urgency becomes real.

Treat big projects like a series of smaller projects. For example, if you're an architect building a house, the first milestone might be to conduct a survey of the land so that you have the most accurate information about topography, soil condition, flood risk, etc. The second milestone might be to identify where on the land to build the house. The third milestone might be to define which rooms are needed, etc.

Worry about what's in front of you—don't worry yet about what's months or years ahead. Then work with your team to set realistic and ambitious target dates for each milestone. Keep in mind the planning fallacy: our natural bias to predict that things will take less time and money than they actually do. Allot a buffer for dealing with unexpected issues.

From your target date, work backward and figure out who needs to do what every week. Ask people to set and publicly commit to their weekly goals—this creates accountability. Periodic reviews can also be a good way to sustain momentum. I know a team who uses this technique expertly, sometimes even hosting two meetings a week to review progress and discuss urgent priorities.

If your team is juggling a number of different tasks, order those by what matters most—which ones are "critical path" and which are "nice to have"? Always tackle "critical path" first.

As it turns out, there are many corollaries to Parkinson's law. My favorite is Mark Horstman's: "Work contracts to fit the time we give it." There is always a way to break down what seems like an impossible journey into a series of days, miles, and finally steps. By putting one foot in front of the other over and over again, eventually we'll scale mountains.

PERFECT EXECUTION OVER PERFECT STRATEGY

I once heard a colleague say that she'd take perfect execution over perfect strategy any day. What's the difference? Well, if your strategy is bad, then you'll make a move on a chessboard that opens you up to attack. But if your execution is bad, then your intended "Rook to E5" somehow becomes "Bishop to D10" because you're trying to play chess with your feet instead of your hands.

The best plans don't matter if you can't achieve them accurately or quickly enough to make a difference. For example, say you had a crystal ball that could tell you the exact industry-disrupting new idea to build. If your end product is slow and buggy compared to the competition, or if you fail to get to market fast enough, you'll still lose the game.

I learned this when I got a chance to see my colleague, whom we'll call Rachel, in action a few years ago. At the time, Rachel and her team defined their road maps in short, multiweek sprint cycles. On week one, Rachel ran a three-hour brainstorm meeting. As the room munched on pizza, goals were proposed and project ideas were scribbled onto the board. Everyone cast their vote for their favorite concepts, and the group narrowed them down to a handful to build.

"But wait a minute," I piped up. I was skeptical that all the ideas would work. And to do some of them well, you'd need months, more time than the sprint allowed. But Rachel explained, "We can either spend the next few weeks debating which ideas are the best or we can try to learn as quickly as possible by *doing*. Our goal is to build simple, conclusive tests that help us understand which things we should double down on and which things we should cut from the list. If an idea works, we'll expand upon it in the next sprint."

Once she said that, I understood why the multiweek cadence was so important. It was short enough that you didn't lose much if any single idea failed. And it was a repeatable process that maximized learnings in the long run.

Throughout your career, you will make countless mistakes. The most frustrating will be the ones where you don't learn anything because it's not clear whether the issue is with strategy or execution.

Every time you see a good script result in a bad movie, a pioneering company lose business to a less innovative competitor, or a genius professor do a poor job of teaching students, you're seeing a failure of execution.

The most brilliant plans in the world won't help you succeed if you can't bring them to life. Executing well means that you pick a reasonable direction, move quickly to learn what works and what doesn't, and make adjustments to get to your desired outcome. Speed matters—a fast runner can take a few wrong turns and still beat a slow runner who knows the shortest path.

Here are some ways to tell if your team is executing well:

- Lists of projects or tasks are prioritized from most to least important, with the higher-up items receiving more time and attention.

- There is an efficient process for decision-making that everyone understands and trusts.

- The team moves quickly, especially with reversible decisions. As Amazon CEO Jeff Bezos says, "Most decisions should probably be made with somewhere around 70% of the information you wish you had. If you wait for 90%, in most cases, you're probably being slow."

- After a decision is made, everyone commits (even those who disagree) and moves speedily to make it happen. Without new information, there is no second-guessing the decision, no pocket vetoing, and no foot dragging.

- When important new information surfaces, there is an expedient process to examine if and how current plans should change as a result.

- Every task has a *who* and a *by when*. Owners set and reliably deliver on commitments.

- The team is resilient and constantly seeking to learn. Every failure makes the team stronger because they don't make the same mistake twice.

Balancing Short-Term and Long-Term Outcomes

Being great at making things happen means recognizing the pragmatic realities of the next day, week, or month as well as the direction you want to steer the ship in the next one, three, or ten years.

It should be clear by now that management is all about the art of balance. When it comes to planning and execution, if you only think about the next three months, you might make shortsighted decisions that create problems down the road. On the flip side, if you're always thinking many years out, you might struggle with speedy day-to-day execution. Here are some common examples of what happens when you tilt too far in one direction or the other.

HIRING

THE SITUATION: You need to hire someone for an important role on your team.

THE RISK OF THINKING TOO SHORT TERM: You say yes to the first person who seems reasonable. While he can do the job now, he's unable to grow with the role. In a year, you find yourself once again with a leadership gap.

THE RISK OF THINKING TOO LONG TERM: Your perfect hire is nearly impossible to find because your bar is so high. You end up rejecting candidate after candidate. Six months later, you still haven't landed someone, and your team's outcomes are suffering.

PLANNING

THE SITUATION: You're a CEO operating in a competitive industry. You need to decide which initiatives to fund.

THE RISK OF THINKING TOO SHORT TERM: You don't make any future investments (like upgrading your equipment) because it's costly in the short term. Meanwhile, your competitors do, and in two years, they're making stuff faster and cheaper than you.

THE RISK OF THINKING TOO LONG TERM: You sign off on a number of three-year projects based on your understanding of today's market. However, a year later, the market has changed, and your plans no longer make sense.

MANAGING PERFORMANCE

THE SITUATION: You're worried that the person you currently have on Project X isn't doing a good job.

THE RISK OF THINKING TOO SHORT TERM: You'll make do with Band-Aid solutions like micromanaging your report or jumping in to work on aspects of the project yourself, neither of which are sustainable.

THE RISK OF THINKING TOO LONG TERM: You invest in coaching your report to improve his performance. However, the changes don't happen quickly, and the project flounders.

As these examples show, you can't always take a blanket short-term or long-term approach. The decisions you make must weigh the trade-offs between the two. So what can you do to find the right balance?

Define a Long-Term Vision and Work Backward

Yogi Berra once said, "If you don't know where you are going, you might wind up someplace else."

Facebook's mission statement is to give people the power to build community and bring the world closer together. In thousands of ways both big and small, this statement is a North Star that guides every team's decision-making.

In 2016, our design team took on the challenge of extending the Like button. The inspiration behind the project came directly from what we heard from users: while people loved the ability to quickly give a thumbs-up to a friend's post, they told us that not everything they saw on Facebook felt "likable." Sometimes, a friend would share that they had had a bad day, and the sentiment they wanted to express was support. Sometimes, they'd encounter news in the world that made them sad or angry. Sometimes, they saw something so genuinely amazing that they wished there was an expression stronger than "like."

Throughout our research, many people gave us suggestions for what we could do. The most common was: "Why don't you build a Dislike button?" It was a logical way to express that something wasn't "likable."

We considered the idea and even came up with a few different designs for how it might work. But, ultimately, we decided it wasn't quite right. Bringing people closer together meant designing experiences that created empathy, and we didn't feel the Dislike button met that bar because it's so easily misinterpreted. If you share, "I went to see Movie X tonight and it didn't live up to the hype," and I "dislike" your post, how should you read my action? Did I also dislike Movie X? Did I dislike that you went to watch Movie X in the first place? Did I dislike that you ragged on what I thought was an awesome movie?

We decided to do more research. When we asked people what they meant when they said, "I wish there was a Dislike button on Facebook," we discovered that they typically wanted to express one of a handful of emotions—sadness, anger, sympathy, or surprise. We took those, as well as the two other most popular sentiments (love and laughter), and developed a system of lightweight reactions to add to the thumbs-up Like. This let people quickly express a wider range of emotions while doing so in a way that stayed true to our mission.

My manager Chris often reminds us, "It's not a good idea to design where your kitchen outlets should go when you haven't yet settled on the floor plan." In other words, start by understanding the bigger picture. What problems are you hoping to solve with what you're doing? How do you imagine people will get value out of your work? Based on that, what are the most important priorities for the team now?

Take a Portfolio Approach

One of the top questions I get from managers is: "How can I carve out time to focus on long-term work when there's so much to do right now to keep the trains running?"

In the framing of this question, there is an assumption that popping your head up to plan for the months or years ahead comes at the expense of successful near-term execution.

It doesn't have to be this way. One of my colleagues runs her team with a strategy that is similar to that of an investor's. Just as no financial advisor would recommend putting all your money into one kind of asset, neither should you tackle projects with one kind of time horizon.

My colleague makes sure that a third of her team works on projects that can be completed on the order of weeks, another third works on medium-term projects that may take months, and finally, the last third works on innovative, early-stage ideas whose impact won't be known for years.

By taking this portfolio approach, her team balances making constant improvements to their core features while casting an eye toward the horizon. Over the past decade, they've shown that this strategy works: her team has an amazing track record of identifying new opportunities and scaling them to huge businesses over the course of three years.

Talk about How Everything Relates to the Vision

If you're part of a larger organization, you'll likely have an overarching vision, whether it's "A chicken in every pot," "Be earth's most customer-centric company" (Amazon's vision), or "Be the most successful and respected car company in America" (Toyota USA's vision). To achieve that, your team will have a specific role to play, whether it's devising a new tax plan, creating the best customer service in the industry, or shooting for close to zero production errors.

It will take months or years to reach your team's aspirations; it may even take decades to fulfill your organization's greater purpose. And yet, if everyone understands and buys into what they are ultimately trying to do, the tactical, day-to-day decisions become easier because you can look at them through the lens of: "Which option moves us closer toward the future that we want?" When people don't understand what ultimately matters and why, that's when conflicts arise.

Early in Facebook's history, Mark Zuckerberg received a billion-dollar offer to sell the company. Looking back, he describes this as his toughest period as a manager. He believed in Facebook's potential to change the world, but he was besieged with pressure from all sides—investors, employees, mentors, and more. "Nearly everyone else wanted to sell," he said while delivering a commencement address at Harvard University in 2017. "Without a sense of higher purpose, this was the start-up dream come true. It tore our company apart. After one tense argument, an advisor told me if I didn't agree to sell, I would regret the decision for the rest of my life."

This was the turning point. Mark made the decision to stay the course and invest in building Facebook's future. He turned down the offer. But the lesson he took away was how important it was to communicate a clear vision and to foster a deep sense of purpose within his team.

At the same time, beware of conflating your purpose with the proxies that you use to measure your progress. For example, if you care about providing the best customer service in the industry, one data point you might track is how long it takes to resolve a customer complaint. Clearly, great customer service correlates with issues getting resolved quickly. Based on that, you might set a goal for the team like, "No customer complaints should take more than three days to close out."

It's a fine goal to set, but don't lose sight of the fact that it's an approximation of what you really care about, which is *providing the best customer service*. If your team focuses too much on this specific goal, you might end up with customer service representatives making hasty calls that go against what the customer wants. If speed of resolution goes up but quality of service goes down, then you're not really getting closer to your vision.

This is why it's so important to remind people of what really matters. Describe over and over again the world you'd like to see. Try to connect every task, project, decision, or goal with the organization's higher-level purpose. If everyone understands the dream, then the team's actions will be aligned in making it a reality.

GOOD PROCESS IS EVER EVOLVING

One of the earliest things I learned about building products, especially digital ones, is that there is no such thing as "finished." You put a version 1.0 out in the world. Then, you learn, you iterate, and you make a better version 2.0 or 3.0. I've gone through countless mobile phones since my first little blue Nokia 3310 in high school. I've changed the pixels on countless iterations of News Feed since its introduction in 2006. What we can achieve is bounded only by the limits of our imagination. If we can dream better, we can do better.

This is true not just for products, but also process. The way we make progress should also be a work in progress.

One of the most useful tools for improving process is the practice of doing debriefs (also called retrospectives or postmortems). You can do this at the completion of a project, on a periodic basis, or anytime an unexpected event or error occurs. Here's how it works: You invite the team to come together for an hour or two to reflect on what happened. What went well, what didn't go well, and what would the team do differently next time?

The process is both cathartic and instructive. There is something to learn even if the outcome was positive (how can we take away best practices for other projects?). If the outcome wasn't good, debriefs help you avoid the same mistakes in the future.

The goal of a debrief is not judgment. Don't treat it as a trial—that's the fastest way to kill the practice. Instead, consider it an opportunity to mine the experience for future lessons. To do this, you must create a safe environment to have open and honest discussions. Present the facts as objectively as possible. ("Here's the timeline: On October 20, Brian and Janice first discussed the possibility of this project. On November 16, they presented the proposal and got the green light to create a new team. . . .") Use language that takes collective accountability instead of pointing fingers ("our process failed . . ." instead of "Leslie made a mistake . . ."), and set the tone that it's okay for us to talk about and learn from our errors.

After a retrospective, it's a good idea to write down the learnings and share them widely. A team growing hardy from its own successes and missteps is great, but when they can also help others improve or avoid similar errors, that's even better. At the end of the day, a resilient organization isn't one that never makes mistakes but rather one whose mistakes make it stronger over time.

Resilient processes also try to create repeatable best practices. Most of the work needed to make something happen in today's world is staggeringly complex. Just imagine the number of steps it takes to get a plane to take off—the cabin must be cleaned from the previous flight, the jet must be refueled, passengers must be checked in, luggage must be loaded, safety checks must be done, and so forth. It's near impossible to remember all the steps in your head, let alone try to improvise them in the moment.

Instead, any feat of complexity—whether it's getting an airplane into the sky, delivering a premature baby, or trying to advance the football down the field—requires a playbook that lays out in clear detail what all the right steps are given the current variables.

As a manager, part of your job will be the cultivation of such playbooks: how to run a team meeting, how to close a new hire, how to complete a project on time and on budget. If you find yourself doing a similar thing over and over again, chances are good that it can be codified into an instruction manual or checklist that can make the task go smoother in the future. Another bonus of doing this: you can then pass the playbook to others to learn and execute.

Some years ago, I started sending out an email to my team summarizing our weekly progress. In the beginning, it was easy for me to sit down, run through all the projects in my head, and jot down the important highlights.

This worked well for a year or so, but as the number of projects doubled and tripled, my process started showing its holes. I'd forget what everyone was doing. On Monday mornings, team members would ping me to ask, "Why didn't you write about my project in the weekly update? Did you not think it was important?"

I was becoming the bottleneck for accurately keeping track of updates. So I came up with a new idea: ask my team to send me what they wanted to highlight for the note. We tried this out, and immediately I felt the burden of needing to remember everything lifted from my shoulders. With my new crowdsourcing technique, I could lean back, relax, and wait for the email to write itself.

Except . . . not quite. The submissions rolled in, but because they were written by many different people, they varied wildly in prose style and level of detail. I had to play the role of editor, taking the snippets and wrangling them so that they sounded as if one person wrote them. Sometimes, when a highlight came in that didn't have enough detail, I'd email the author and we'd go back and forth to improve it. My new process solved some major problems but created new ones—namely that it still took me a really long time to put together the weekly email.

Enter phase three: I realized I was frequently giving the same feedback over and over again, so I created a document called *How to Submit a Highlight for the Weekly Digest*. In it, I listed the goals of the digest, what made for a good highlight, and tips to keep in mind while writing. I shared it with the folks on my team as well as with new people after they joined.

Phase three seems to be working for now, but I expect that, as things change, even small processes like this will continue to evolve. The next chapter goes into more detail about how to manage a growing team.

This book itself is the latest iteration of my personal playbook, the culmination of years of failing, succeeding, and trying in the endeavor known as management. I'm writing it for you, but I'm also writing it for myself—so that I can remember the mistakes I've made and the lessons I've tucked away for the future.

Heraclitus, the Greek philosopher, once said: "No man ever steps in the same river twice, for it is not the same river and he is not the same man." Every challenge is like crossing such a river. Investigate the stepping-stones, the currents, the hidden eddies. And then, once you make your plan, take that first step to get to the other side.

In the process of navigating that river, you might slip. You might fall in. You might have to start over again. But, hopefully, you are made wiser. Take a moment to reflect on what you've learned and how you might plan that next crossing. And may you boldly saunter across rushing water the next time it meets your path.

Chapter Nine

Leading a Growing Team

Back when we still fit around a conference room table, a new designer joining our merry band was a momentous event. Everyone loved sitting down and showing her how we worked—where we kept our design files, what tools to download, which meetings to attend. We were grateful that someone else had come to help us accomplish more together. Even better, the newcomer brought additional superpowers, whether it was an eagle eye for visuals, a deep understanding of human motivation, or an uncanny ability to propose out-of-the-box ideas. Our critique group pulled up an extra chair and expanded its perspective. Two pizzas were still enough to feed everyone.

A few months later, another new person would join. And another. And another. And each time, the process repeated itself—new faces and superpowers were introduced to the current team and our existing processes.

Until one day, you wake up and realize the old ways no longer work.

The turning point for me was walking into critique one day and realizing that, all of a sudden, our regular room didn't have enough seats for everyone. This wasn't a big deal in and of itself—a few helpful folks quickly went out and brought back some extra chairs—but when we made the list of everyone who wanted to share, it was ten people long. In the past, we were lucky if we could get through even five or six projects in a single meeting!

This meant that half of those who volunteered wouldn't get a chance to present that day. Since critique's whole purpose was to be a reliable forum for design feedback, something had to change.

And it wasn't just that one meeting. My own days were getting squeezed with the need to support our team's growth. There were more unexpected issues that kept popping up, more announcements to communicate, more decisions to keep track of. This pattern kept repeating itself. As soon as I figured out a better process, a few more people would join and the gears would get clogged once more. The only way to stay effective was to constantly change and adapt.

When I first began managing, my team was only a handful of people. And then it doubled. Every few years, it doubled again. At each of those points, I felt like I had an entirely different job. While the core principles of management stayed the same, the day-to-day changed significantly.

Your frontline view of how a team works starts to evolve into a macro view. Setting a vision, hiring leaders, delegating responsibility, and managing communication become the key skills needed to bridge the gap. In this chapter, we'll look at the differences you'll experience and how to make the leap.

BIG TEAMS VERSUS SMALL TEAMS

In Silicon Valley, hyper-growth is almost a way of life. The siren song of an ambitious dream can cause teams to expand at a dizzying pace. Career pages list dozens of roles; weekly orientations greet a sea of new faces. It's common to feel that change and chaos are the only constants; everything else is improvisation. I tell prospective employees that a major reason why I love my job is this quality—with new challenges popping up every day, opportunities to learn are everywhere I look.

People often ask me what's different about my job now than

when I started. Looking back, these are the most striking contrasts between managing small and large teams.

Direct to Indirect Management

If your team is five people, you can develop a personal relationship with each individual where you understand the details of their work, what they care about and are good at, and maybe even the hobbies they enjoy outside of the office.

If your team is thirty people, you can't manage them all directly, at least, not to the same degree. If you did weekly thirty-minute 1:1s with everyone, that alone would take fifteen hours—about half of the workweek! Add in time to follow up on any action items from those conversations, and you'd barely be able to do anything else. When I got to more than eight reports, I started to feel like I didn't have enough hours in the day to support everyone well while also thinking about hiring, ensuring high-quality design work, and contributing to product strategy.

This is why managers of growing teams eventually start to hire or develop managers underneath them. But this means you're further removed from the people and the work on the ground. You're still responsible for your team's outcomes, but you can't be in all the details. Decisions will be made without your input, and things will be done differently than how you might personally do them.

At first, this can feel disorienting, like you're losing control. But empowering your leaders is a necessity. One of the biggest challenges of managing at scale is finding the right balance between going deep on a problem and stepping back and trusting others to take care of it. More on that topic in a bit.

People Treat You Differently

Some years ago, when my team had grown beyond the point where I knew everybody personally, I attended a review where three designers who reported up through me presented their latest work. I gave them my feedback and asked for a follow-up review the next week. Before we ended, I asked if there were any thoughts or questions about what I had said. Everyone shook their heads. I left thinking that it was, all in all, a good and productive meeting.

Later in the day, I saw one of my direct reports who also happened to be in that meeting. He wore a grave look on his face. "I caught up with the team and they're not feeling good about the review this morning," he told me. I thought he was joking. "What? Why?" "They didn't agree with your feedback," he said. "But why didn't they tell me that?" I asked incredulously. My report paused. "Well, Julie, you're kind of a big deal, so they were intimidated."

It was the first time I'd ever heard anyone refer to me as "kind of a big deal." It was hard to compute. When did I become the kind of person who intimidated others? I'd always prided myself on my approachability.

What I learned is that it didn't matter how I saw myself. When people don't know you well and see that you're in a position of authority, they're less likely to tell you the ugly truth or challenge you when they think you're wrong, even if you'd like them to. They might think it's your prerogative to call the shots. They might not want to disappoint you or have you think badly of them. Or they might be trying to make your life easier by not burdening you with new problems or imposing on your time.

Be aware of this dynamic in your interactions with others. Are your suggestions being taken as orders? Are your questions coming off as judgments? Are you presuming that things are rosier than they really are because you're not hearing the full story?

Happily, there are some countermeasures you can take to

make it easier for people to tell you the truth. Emphasize that you welcome dissenting opinions and reward those who express them. Own your mistakes and remind your team that you are human, just like everyone else. Use language that invites discussion: "I may be totally wrong here, so tell me if you disagree. My opinion is . . ." You can also ask directly for advice: "If you were me, what would you do in this situation?"

Context Switching All Day, Every Day

When I managed a small team, I spent many afternoons with a handful of designers at the whiteboard, exploring new ideas. So deep would we get into the flow of our work that hours would pass in the blink of an eye.

As my team grew, my capacity to spend long, focused blocks on a single topic began to shrink. More people meant that we could tackle more projects, which meant that my time broke into smaller and smaller fragments. Ten emails would come into my inbox about ten completely different topics. Back-to-back meetings required me to immediately shed the past discussion and get mentally prepared for the next one.

When I didn't do this well, I'd be distracted and overwhelmed, my mind constantly jumping from one topic to another. I'd lose focus during presentations. I'd mutter that *every day felt like a week*.

Over time, I came to understand that this *was* the job. As the number of projects I was responsible for doubled, tripled, and quadrupled, my ability to context switch also needed to keep pace. I discovered a few techniques to make this easier: scanning through my calendar every morning and preparing for each meeting, developing a robust note-taking and task-management system, finding pockets for reflection at the end of every week. Some days I'm still distracted. But I've come to accept that there will always be a dozen different issues to work through at any given time—some big, some small, and some unexpected—and as the manager of a large team, you learn to roll with it.

You Pick and Choose Your Battles

When I managed a small team, there were days when I'd close my laptop and walk out of the office with zero outstanding tasks left—my inbox was cleared, my to-dos were crossed off, and nothing else needed my attention. As my scope grew, those days became rarer and rarer until they ceased to exist completely.

It's a game of numbers, after all. The more you look after, the more likely it is that something under your purview isn't going as well as it could be. It might be projects falling behind schedule, miscommunications that need clearing up, or people who aren't getting what they need. At any given moment, I can list dozens of areas that I could be working to improve.

But at the end of the day, you are only one individual with a limited amount of time. You can't do everything, so you must prioritize. What are the most important topics for you to pay attention to, and where are you going to draw the line? Perfectionism is not an option. It took me a long time to get comfortable operating in a world where I had to pick and choose what mattered the most, and not let the sheer number of possibilities overwhelm me.

The Skills That Matter Become More and More People-Centric

I remember hearing about a CEO who made the executives on his team switch roles every few years, like a game of musical chairs. I was skeptical. It seemed like one of those tall tales meant to illustrate a point about the importance of workplace empathy. But really, now. How could a sales executive be expected to know how to run an engineering organization or a chief financial officer be a strong chief marketing officer?

Nowadays, I don't think an executive swap is as far-fetched as I once thought. As teams grow, managers spend less of their day-to-day on the specific craft of their discipline. What matters more is that they can get the best out of a group of people. For example, no CEO is an expert across sales and design, engineering and communications, finance and human resources. And yet, she is tasked with building and leading an organization that does all of these things.

At higher levels of management, the job starts to converge regardless of background. Success becomes more and more about mastering a few key skills: hiring exceptional leaders, building self-reliant teams, establishing a clear vision, and communicating well.

THE TIGHTROPE ACT OF GREAT DELEGATION

For me, the most rewarding part of growing my team has been watching our collective capabilities extend far beyond what any one of us could have achieved. But on the flip side, the hardest part has been learning how to effectively delegate, which I define as "the art of knowing when to dive in yourself and when to step back and entrust others." Like crossing a tightrope while blindfolded, the balance is difficult to sustain.

At each extreme, you've become a sitcom cliché: Dive in too much, and you're the micromanager. You ask your reports to run every decision by you. You're constantly checking in with people, asking for status updates and diving in to the minutiae of tasks. *Did John correct the last statement yet? When is the China shipment coming in? I don't like the shade of blue on this packaging.* You have a reputation for prowling behind people's desks and giving your opinion about what's on their screens.

Even if you get results, your style is stifling. Talented people leave because they can't stand working for you. They don't feel that you give them trust or breathing room to operate. And they're not learning because they don't get a chance to solve problems on their own. Rumor has it that what you really want is an army of robots to do your bidding.

At the other extreme, if you step back too much, you're the absentee manager. Some of your reports appreciate the independence, but most wish they had more support. When things get rocky, your team feels like the Wild West, a place with no rules because there's no sheriff in town.

Your hands are pristine because you rarely roll up your sleeves and get into the nitty-gritty. You don't make hard calls or proactively push things forward. Over time, you lose credibility as a leader because . . . well, you don't do much. And your reports aren't learning because you're not coaching or challenging them. People whisper that maybe you aren't really there at all—you're simply *overhead*.

Of course, in the real world, we're rarely at the extremes. But we do tend to lean one way or the other based on our values. For example, as a new manager, I was on the absentee side of the spectrum because I personally disliked being micromanaged. Then, when I got feedback that my reports wanted me to be more hands-on, I overcorrected and then heard: "Okay, too much!"

It's also common to lean different ways in different aspects of the job depending on where your team is. For example, in the span of a week, one report gave me feedback that I was too opinionated about a specific design detail, while another report asked me to get more involved with the strategy of a separate project. Each needed different things—one was confident in what he was doing, so my involvement seemed overbearing. The other wasn't, and so wanted more of my help.

In the moment, you don't always know how you're doing on the balance. I've had situations where I've stepped back in an area thinking, *This is going fine so I'm going to focus on something else.* Then, a few weeks later, I realized that I hadn't set up the work well and that I should have remained closer to the details.

Delegating well is far from an exact science, but there are a few guiding principles that we'll explore next.

GIVING PEOPLE BIG PROBLEMS IS A SIGN OF TRUST

Growing up, I had the kind of grandmother who would gladly do anything to make my life easier. When I went outside to play on a winter's day, she'd run out waving a sweater and yelling my name. When I came home from school, there would be a beautiful plate of snacks waiting for me. When I struggled with basic tasks—opening a box of markers, figuring out where the next puzzle piece should go, or getting a book from a top shelf—she'd drop whatever she was doing and say, "Here, let me."

On the one hand, I knew she was doing these things out of a fierce love. She didn't want to see me go through any hardships. But on the other hand, I found myself wishing that she wouldn't. We joke now about how I used to yell at her, "Go away! Don't help me!" when she'd materialize like a fairy godmother with some food or clothing or a spare hand. I wanted her love and support, but like all kids, I craved independence. I wanted the freedom to deal with my own issues my way.

With this background, you'd think that I'd be more clear-headed in my approach to delegation. But no, I thought that it was the *bad* managers who gave hard problems to their reports. I imagined them lazing about, sipping wine after a morning round of golf. Great managers, in my mind, were like my grandmother—they took on the biggest burdens of the team to spare their reports.

There are two major errors with that line of thinking. The first is overestimating what you, the manager, are capable of. Yes, it may be within your power to solve a wide variety of issues, but as a single individual, you can't solve *that many* of them. The best work comes from those who have the time to live and breathe a problem fully, who can dedicate themselves to finding the best solution.

The second error is assuming that nobody wants to take on hard problems. In fact, the most talented employees aren't looking for special treatment or "easy" projects. They *want* to be challenged. There is no greater sign of trust than handing your report an intricately tangled knot that you believe she can pull apart, even if you're not sure how.

The key, of course, is that you need to *actually* believe your report is capable of solving the problem. If that's the case, give it to her and step back so she has the space to lead. Tell everyone else that she should now be considered the owner of the problem. Doing so creates accountability, but more important, the public declaration empowers the delegate. For example, imagine a CEO asking an employee, Elaine, to be in charge of managing the company's finances. To be effective, Elaine needs everyone to respect the budget she sets and provide the financial information she needs. Will Elaine have an easier time if the CEO tells the entire company, "Elaine is our chief financial officer," or if he privately asks her to do this without letting anyone else know?

Delegating a hard problem doesn't mean you simply walk away. Just like you wouldn't toss a novice swimmer into the deep end of the pool while you go and get a snack, you shouldn't leave your report to fend for himself. He's the captain, but you're with him on the boat. You're rooting him on, helping him with whatever he needs you to do, and coaching him so he can smoothly and safely sail to his destination.

TWO HEADS, ONE SHARED VISION

When I was just starting out, I thought that a manager could only be effective if she knew everything that was going on. How else could you make good decisions or give relevant feedback? In 1:1s, I'd ask my reports for status updates. We'd go through the latest design work, the product debates of the moment, and the timelines and expectations for the next week.

We never had enough time to cover everything. It turns out that doing this kind of knowledge transfer during 1:1s is poor management practice for many reasons. One-on-ones aren't for the manager's benefit; they should be about what's helpful for the other person. Also, it's unrealistic to expect that you should know all the details of your report's day-to-day, especially as your team grows and your reports are managers juggling their own long lists of responsibilities.

What you *should* expect is that you see eye to eye on what's most important. The historian Yuval Noah Harari, in his bestselling book *Sapiens*, theorizes that the one unique trait that made the human species the most successful in the world is that we are able to share the same vision in our heads, which helps even complete strangers work together. "We control the world basically because we are the only animals that can cooperate flexibly in very large numbers," says Harari.

To create a shared vision of what's important, ask yourself two things. The first is, *What are the biggest priorities right now for our team?* Then, talk about those with your reports and discuss how they might play a role. For example, if the company is in the midst of executing a new strategy, talk about why that's happening and how your teams will be affected. Similarly, if an impending launch is keeping you up at night, you and your reports should discuss how everyone can do their part to ensure things go smoothly.

Once these top priorities are covered, ask yourself the second question: *Are we aligned in how we think about people, purpose, and process?*

Digging in one level deeper, does your report know what matters to you when it comes to team building? Does he understand what you expect of him as a coach for his own reports? Do you see eye to eye on which of his team members are knocking it out of the park and which aren't meeting expectations?

Once, a few colleagues and I put together a project update for my manager Chris at a review meeting. Our news was bleak—some recent product launches hadn't gone as well as we'd hoped, and the team was feeling drained. We walked into the room bracing ourselves for a serious talk about the state of affairs. Instead, Chris said, "So there's a lot going on, but what I'm most interested in is the team. Do we feel like we have the right people on the right problems?" His question cut through the noise and reminded us of what mattered most. People trump projects—a great team is a prerequisite for great work.

Beyond people, you and your report should be aligned on why you're doing what you're doing and what success looks like. As Antoine de Saint-Exupéry has been attributed as saying, "If you want to build a ship, don't drum up the men to gather wood, divide the work, and give orders. Instead, teach them to yearn for the vast and endless sea."

This week's tasks, meetings, and emails will be little blips lost in the sands of time. What is the greater purpose behind them? Why do you get out of bed every morning and come to work? What will be different about the world if your team achieves its goals? Constantly talking about the purpose with your reports makes it more vivid in everyone's minds. When the vision is clear, the right actions tend to follow.

Lastly, are your reports establishing healthy processes for their teams? Whether it's advice on how to pitch new ideas, best practices for communicating important updates, discussions on meeting dos and don'ts—my reports tell me that whenever we talk about how to best get things done, it always feels like a valuable use of time.

WHAT TO DO WHEN A MANAGER STRUGGLES

What should you do if one of the managers on your team isn't meeting the expectations of her role? You might think, *My job is to support her and help her through it.* You're not wrong. After all, we just talked about how important it is to empower your leaders to tackle hard problems. If the bar is perfection, nobody is even going to try. Part of delegating well is recognizing that your reports—like you—will make mistakes and doubt themselves, and that often the best thing you can do is to believe in them.

But the full answer is more nuanced. A manager's job is to be a positive multiplier for her team. When she isn't, the costs are high: projects take longer because she inserts herself at the wrong times, outcomes are poor because she makes bad calls, or complaints pile up because her people aren't getting what they need.

Even when a manager isn't actively making things worse, she may still be holding the team back. Maybe she can put out fires but she's not helping the team become more fireproof. Or she can fill roles but not attract the best talent. Or maybe she requires more coaching to be effective than you have time to give.

At fast-scaling organizations, it's common for new teams to

form almost overnight to tackle new challenges. Early on, those teams are small and scrappy, so any manager hired is expected to oversee a handful of people and a few speculative projects.

Now, fast-forward two or three years. Due to a mix of ingenuity, hard work, and luck, some of those speculative projects become hugely successful. The teams behind them grow rapidly to keep pace. That original manager, perfect for an early-stage team, is now grappling with the challenges of leading a much bigger group. What was once a smoothly sailing ship now feels as though it's pitching back and forth against a wild storm.

In those situations, I'd find myself at a crossroads. Of course I believed in the manager. He might need to improve certain skills, but I knew he'd eventually get there. I myself went through those very same choppy waters. The growth mindset taught me that anyone can get better at anything given the will, hard work, and time. The question was, how long would it take? And how would that affect the team?

Once, as I was working through those questions with a report we'll call Raphael, I turned to the words of Andy Grove: "The subordinate did poor work. My associate's reaction: 'He has to make his own mistakes. That's how he learns!' The problem with this is that the subordinate's tuition is paid by his customers. And that is absolutely wrong."

Andy reminded me that the end goal of management is to *get better outcomes*. When someone isn't a great fit for his role, there is a cost. Would you rather pay it by making a hard move or by passing it on to other team members and customers?

A friend of mine gave me the gift of another clarifying question. He asked: "Assume the role was open. Would you rather rehire your current leader or take a gamble on someone else?"

This question helped me to zero in on what really mattered. Here I was, worried about dozens of details—how Raphael would feel, whether or not I was giving him enough feedback, the thrash everyone else would go through—when the most important question was, *What's going to make the team more successful over the next few years?*

The following week, I sat down with Raphael and told him that I felt he should move off his current role. The conversation wasn't easy, but looking back now, I know that it was the right call. The new manager who came in afterward had a wealth of experience running bigger teams. Like a seasoned captain who had sailed all over the world, he sauntered up to the wheel and steered the ship out of the storm. After a few months of transition, the team thrived and its work improved.

Change is hard, but trust your instincts. Would you hire this person again if the role were open? If the answer is no, make the move.

AIM TO PUT YOURSELF OUT OF A JOB

The best managers I know all agree on one thing: growing great teams means that you are constantly looking for ways to replace yourself in the job you are currently doing.

For example, if you're responsible for solving Problem X and you can find or train someone to do it as well as you (or, ideally, *better* than you), then your team as a whole becomes more capable and you personally can take on more. A friend of mine states it as a simple rule of thumb: "Try to double your leadership capacity every year."

This sounds nice in theory but is harder to do in practice because we have a tendency to get attached to what we're doing. We may love the task itself or the sense of expertise and control it gives us.

Every Monday, I used to run a company-wide design meeting. I had come up with the idea when the team was still small, so I managed the agenda and played the role of emcee. I was proud of this weekly ritual when all the designers gathered around to hear the latest updates, see examples of inspiring work, and welcome the newest members of the team. And, to be honest, it felt nice to be in charge and see the fruits of my labor.

But the point of being a manager is not to satisfy your own ego; it's to improve the outcomes of your team. In the early days, I saw a need for us to share lessons and build community, so I initiated the meeting. I didn't think anybody else would do it. Years later, this was no longer the case. We had plenty of new leaders who could run that meeting.

I ended up delegating it accidentally. During my parental leave, I asked a few of my teammates to sub for me while I was out. When I came back, the meeting was running better than I'd left it. The presenters came in more prepared, the content was better organized, and even our introductions felt more fun.

That was when I realized my mistake. I should have handed off that meeting a long time ago. I felt tied to it because it had become habitual, even a part of my identity. And yet, in my absence, the organizers breathed new life into it. They were excited for the challenge, and I was able to focus on other priorities. Everybody won.

The rule of thumb for delegation goes like this: spend your time and energy on the intersection of 1) what's most important to the organization and 2) what you're uniquely able to do better than anyone else.

From this, you can extrapolate that anything your report can do just as well or better than you, you should delegate.

Some time ago, a few of my reports suggested that we do more to strengthen relationships within our team. They noticed people scurrying from meeting to meeting and from home to work without really getting to know each other. Couldn't we do more to build community? What about events like group lunches, show-

and-tell learning sessions, or mentorship circles? I loved all the suggestions. But, personally, this wasn't my strong suit. (After we got engaged, my fiancé learned that planning social events like a wedding ranks among my least favorite activities in the world.)

Happily, other folks on the team were the exact opposite, including the manager who had kicked off the discussion. He loved meeting new people and rallying groups together, so I asked him to take charge of figuring out what we should do. One of his ideas, a monthly Wednesday-night mixer, grew so popular that it expanded beyond our team to become a regular meet-and-greet for the local design community.

For the things that you do better than your reports, unless it falls into the "most important priorities" bucket or you don't believe they are set up to succeed, you should still try to delegate as much as possible and coach them along the way. For example, because I've managed longer, I'm more comfortable having hard conversations than some newer leaders on my team. Does that mean that whenever anyone needs to hear a tough message, I should be the one delivering it? Definitely not. It's better if everyone can collectively improve their feedback skills over time.

This is a classic example of short-term versus long-term trade-offs. If your report presents you a problem that you can easily solve, it can be difficult to resist saying, "I'll take care of it." But as the proverb goes, give someone a fish, and you feed them for a day. Teach someone to fish, and you feed them for a lifetime.

As for what you shouldn't delegate, consider the unique value you're able to add when it comes to the organization's top priorities. Some of that flows from your personal strengths. For example, I'm a good writer, so over the years I've used that skill to help our team document and share its values—from authoring career guidelines and interview playbooks to putting out internal notes on lessons we've learned in building products. One of my colleagues is an amazing operator, so he's responsible for running our design team's most complex processes, such as recruiting. My manager Chris is one of the most inspiring speakers I know, so he's the first person to greet new employees at orientation and tell them about Facebook's mission and values.

Beyond your individual superpowers, there are a few other patterns that lie at the intersection of "important to the organization" and "you can add unique value."

Identifying and communicating what matters. Your role has broader scope, which means that you're able to see across a wider variety of work and spot patterns that your reports might miss.

A few years ago, I noticed that some of our recent launches had design elements that were trying to do the same thing but looked and behaved differently. For example, a button would be dark blue and rectangular in one part of the product, but light blue and oval in another. A Back button might be at the top of the page in some instances but at the bottom in others. This had the effect of making our product feel harder to use because there weren't predictable patterns that people could rely on. Seeing this, I rallied our team to establish a common design pattern library so that we'd all work off the same building blocks. As we scaled, this library became an increasingly important tool to help us move quickly and cohesively.

Hiring top talent. Because prospective candidates are generally interested in talking with senior leaders, you have an advantage when it comes to finding and closing talent. I attend industry events and speak at conferences so that I can attract people to our team. I tell my reports that if they have a candidate they're excited about, I'm happy to send that person a note or offer to talk on the phone. My manager does the same for me. No matter if you are the CEO or a front-line manager, building a great team is one of the most important things you can do.

Resolving conflicts within my group. Imagine that there are two separate projects managed by two of your reports, both of which are understaffed. A new person wants to join your team. Which project should he work on?

You can't ask your reports to sort this out and come back to you with a recommendation because neither has the full perspective on what matters most. They'll waste time trying to convince each other why their project really needs that new person. The decision has to be made by you. Make sure your leaders know to quickly escalate to you whenever two goals come into conflict or when the priorities aren't clear.

Once, as I was describing the philosophy of always looking to put yourself out of a job, a report asked me: "Okay, but if you *did* delegate everything to others, doesn't that mean you become overhead? Why would you still be valuable?"

It was an excellent question, and one I've asked before as well. In response, I said, "If you delegated everything you did today to someone else, do you think there'd be no more problems left for you to solve?"

Today, my job looks very different than when I started. Every time I've given a piece of it away, I've discovered that there was ever more to take on. As long as you continue to be motivated by your purpose, as long as your aspirations extend beyond what your team is currently capable of, as long as you can see new challenges on the horizon, then there's opportunity for you to have more impact. Often, this means doing new things that you're not very good at yet. Compared to the expertise you had in the responsibilities you delegated away, this can feel uncomfortable.

And yet, as your team grows in its size and abilities, so too must you grow to keep pace as its manager. The act of constantly trying to replace yourself means that you create openings to stretch both your leaders and yourself. Right ahead is another mountain that's bigger and scarier than the one before. Everyone keeps climbing, and everyone achieves more together.

Chapter Ten
Nurturing Culture

AVOID

ASPIRE

Whenever I ask prospective candidates if they have any questions for me, inevitably we get to talking about culture: "What's unique about your team?" "What are the best and worst parts of your job?" "How are decisions made?" "If you could change one thing about the way the company works, what would that be?"

A manager I admire once told me that an organization's culture is best understood not from reading what's written on its corporate website but from seeing what it's willing to give up for its values. For example, many teams say that they care about their employees fully owning problems. Nobody's going to admit, "Actually, we like to shirk responsibility and blame mistakes on others."

But operating with full ownership has its trade-offs. Are you willing to tolerate the chaos that comes from everyone trying to do what they think is best? Can you appreciate when other people challenge your decisions? Are you okay accepting responsibility for mistakes that aren't directly your own? At Facebook, we have a saying immortalized in posters all across campus: *Nothing at Facebook Is Somebody Else's Problem.*

One summer, a new intern took down the Facebook service by accidentally introducing a bad error into the codebase. As everyone worked madly to fix the mistake, I caught a glimpse of his ashen face. I'm sure he thought he was going to be fired.

He wasn't. His manager apologized instead for not setting him up better. Other engineers took accountability for not catching the error beforehand. The entire team then participated in a post-mortem to understand why the failure happened and what changes could be made to prevent similar issues in the future.

Culture describes the norms and values that govern how things get done. A manager I was mentoring once shared with me his epiphany about the job three years in. "At first, I thought management was about supporting the individuals who reported to me," he said. "I focused on creating the best one-on-one relationships I could. But now I realize that isn't enough. Because it's not just about *my* relationship to the team. It's also about their relationships with each other, and with the group as a whole."

As you manage more and more people, you'll play a bigger role in shaping culture. Don't underestimate the influence that you can have. Even if you're not the CEO, your actions reinforce what the company values. The next few sections guide you through how to establish the kind of culture that you're proud of.

KNOW THE KIND OF TEAM YOU WANT TO BE A PART OF

Your team's culture is like its personality. It exists whether or not you think about it. If you're not satisfied with how your team works together—maybe the vibe feels hostile instead of helpful, maybe it takes a long time to get things done, or maybe there's constant drama—it's worth examining why this might be and what you can do about it.

Remember the exercises from Chapter Five: Managing Yourself when we wrote down your personal strengths, growth areas, and aspirations? It's time to do the same with your team. The key is to find the intersection between what your team does well and what you hope the team values. When you have an hour or so, grab a pen and jot down your answers to the following questions:

UNDERSTANDING YOUR CURRENT TEAM

- What are the first three adjectives that come to mind when describing the personality of your team?
- What moments made you feel most proud to be a part of your team? Why?
- What does your team do better than the majority of other teams out there?
- If you picked five random members of your team and individually asked each person, "What does our team value?" what would you hear?
- How similar is your team's culture to the broader organization's culture?
- Imagine a journalist scrutinizing your team. What would she say your team does well or not well?
- When people complain about how things work, what are the top three things that they bring up?

UNDERSTANDING YOUR ASPIRATIONS

- Describe the top five adjectives you'd want an external observer to use to describe your team's culture. Why those?
- Now imagine those five adjectives sitting on a double-edged sword. What do you imagine are the pitfalls that come from ruthless adherence to those qualities? Are those acceptable to you?
- Make a list of the aspects of culture that you admire about other teams or organizations. Why do you admire them? What downsides does that team tolerate as a result?
- Make a list of the aspects of culture that you wouldn't want to emulate from other teams or companies. Why not?

UNDERSTANDING THE DIFFERENCE

- On a scale from one to nine, with nine being "we're 100 percent there" and one being "this is the opposite of our team," how close is your current team from your aspirations?
- What shows up as both a strength of your team as well as a quality you value highly?
- Where are the biggest gaps between your current team culture and your aspirations?
- What are the obstacles that might get in the way of reaching your aspirations? How will you address them?
- Imagine how you want your team to work in a year's time. How would you describe to a report what you hope will be different then compared to now?

Depending on what's within your control, some of your aspirations may be doable and some unrealistic. For example, if you want your team to operate with utter focus and zero distractions, you might prefer they sit in a remote area and avoid interacting with other groups. But if the broader company values openness and collaboration, your preference would be hard to achieve.

That said, subcultures can grow and flourish within a larger organization. For example, Facebook's growth team values being rigorously data informed. Our infrastructure engineering team is known for its long-term focus. And within design, we care about finding holistic solutions to problems.

Once you've identified the values you want to nurture within your team, the next step is to develop a game plan to help those values flourish.

NEVER STOP TALKING ABOUT WHAT'S IMPORTANT

When I first started managing, I considered it bad form to repeat myself. I figured that my team would find it annoying, and perhaps even condescending, if I said the same thing over and over again.

Sheryl Sandberg was the one who taught me otherwise. Some years ago, Sheryl started talking to the company about the importance of hard conversations. Whenever we're feeling tension with our coworkers—they have a habit that irritates us, we disagree about an important decision, or they do something that seems thoughtless—she encouraged us to sit down with the other person and discuss that tension openly. Because if you don't, nothing will get better, and resentment will only grow.

I can't recall exactly when Sheryl started talking about hard conversations, and that's precisely the point. It could have been during one of our company-wide meetings, or during a Q&A, or during a dinner hosted at her house. She would ask people to raise their hands if they'd had a hard conversation in the past month. She'd then tell us a story about one of her recent hard conversations.

"Hard conversations" became part of the vernacular at Facebook because Sheryl believed so strongly that it was critical for a healthy company culture. To this day, whenever I feel tension knotting in my stomach—a misunderstanding that's gone on for too long, a concern about a strategy, a sense that a coworker is upset with me—I think of Sheryl. Then I square my shoulders and invite that person for a heart-to-heart chat.

When you value something deeply, don't shy away from talking about it. Instead, embrace telling people why it's important to you. Assume that for the message to stick, it should be heard ten different times and said in ten different ways. The more you can enlist others to help spread your message, the more likely it is to have an impact.

These days, I think a lot about how to communicate what I care about. I try different approaches—1:1 conversations about what's on my mind, emails to my managers about my reflections for the week, notes to my entire staff on our top priorities, and in-person Q&A sessions focused on how we work.

I've found that the more frequently and passionately I talk about what's important to me—including my missteps and what I've learned through them—the more positively my team responds. I'll get notes from people saying, "I care about that too. How can I help?" I'll hear others reinforcing the same messages and supporting each other to change their behavior. And even when people disagree with me, the act of discussing it openly sheds light on the topic for everyone.

As I've given greater voice to what I care about, nobody, not even once, has told me that it's annoying or condescending. Instead, the feedback is the opposite—talking about your values makes you a more authentic and inspiring leader.

ALWAYS WALK THE WALK

People watch their bosses closely to understand the team's values and norms. Our radars are fine-tuned to spot instances where someone in a position of authority says one thing and does another. This is one of the fastest ways to lose trust. Consider the following examples:

- A manager asks his team to spend company money wisely, but then splurges on a fancy desk and couch for his office.
- A manager expresses annoyance when her report shows up

after a meeting has already started, but she herself is five minutes late to everything.

- A manager says he wants more diverse perspectives on the team but only promotes people who think like him.
- A manager says a top goal is to create a supportive work environment, but she has a tendency to lose her temper and chew out her reports.
- A CEO says that the goal of his company is to serve a social mission, but his decisions read like they are favoring short-term profits.

If you're not willing to change your behavior for a stated value, then don't bring it up in the first place.

I experienced this lesson the hard way. Once, a report asked me in a 1:1 what I believed was the best way for her to accelerate her learning. She was bright-eyed and fiercely determined, the kind of person who never met an obstacle she couldn't overcome. Delighted by the question, I responded, "Ask for feedback." I then spent the rest of the 1:1 describing how important I considered feedback to be, along with some suggestions for how she could proactively seek it out. Maybe she could show her designs to trusted colleagues outside of critique or ask for a few quick takes on how well she presented following a review. My report nodded along.

Because she was so motivated, I expected to see her try out these tactics right away and ask me and others for more feedback. But I saw no change.

A few weeks later, we all went through 360 reviews. This report shared her feedback with me directly. She gave some good suggestions around communication and prioritization. At the very end, she included this bullet: "You rarely ask me or others on the team for feedback, and I'd love to see you do more of it."

It was eye opening. I realized that as much as I talked about the importance of asking for feedback, I wasn't living it myself. And she noticed! Chastened, I resolved to keep practicing until it became habitual.

If you say something is important to you and you'd like the rest of your team to care about it, be the first person to live that value. Otherwise, don't be surprised when nobody else does either.

CREATE THE RIGHT INCENTIVES

Let's say you talk the talk and walk the walk. That means all your cultural aspirations will come true, right? Not quite. The final piece is ensuring that your environment rewards people who behave according to your team's values and holds people accountable when they don't.

If the incentives don't match—if, say, you care a lot about operating with transparency but your team believes they will be better off if they conceal important information from you—you need to dig deeper to understand what's sending that message. What actions or results does your team celebrate, and where does it draw the line?

Sometimes, even the best intentions can lead to bad incentives. Some years ago, I noticed that during design critique, most of the room was showing just one design exploration for a given problem. This wasn't ideal because the best solutions tend to come from trying many different ideas. If you say "good enough" to the first thing that pops into your head, you're probably leaving better options undiscovered.

The following week, I asked everyone to bring in at least three different explorations of whatever they were working on. Thinking this was a brilliant way to encourage more creativity, I eagerly awaited our next critique.

The first designer to present showed the room a simple promotion describing a new feature we were about to launch. "Here's what I came up with," he said. There was a graphic sitting next to some text, with a blue button to learn more. We nodded along—it was a solid design. "Here are some other variations as well, since we were asked to show at least three options." He then flipped through a few more images where he changed the positioning of the text and graphic and made the button a different color. Each version was clearly worse than the original. "Why are we considering an orange button here when all the other buttons on our site are blue?" someone asked. "That doesn't really make sense."

As the critique went on, it became clear that my "show three explorations" rule also wasn't making sense. While some people ended up with a wider range of interesting ideas, others went through the motions of changing things just for the sake of it, not because they were excited about the new options. This created busywork and wasted everybody's time.

I hear similar stories of bad incentives in other fields. A well-known example in engineering is tracking lines of code and rewarding engineers who write the most. While it seems logical at first glance—*this is going to encourage everyone to work harder and write programs faster!*—in practice, what you get is bloated, copy-and-paste code rather than neat, elegant functions. The equivalent in writing is paying an author by the word, which would make sense if longer novels always made for better reading. Hemingway may beg to differ.

These days, I'm wary of seemingly simple incentive rules that promise amazing results. They are rarely simple, and often leave collateral damage. Usually, a better option is to have a frank discussion about what we should value and *why*. Why should we care about exploring more designs early on? Why should we aim to speed up engineering velocity? Once people understand and buy into those values, they can make the best decisions on how to apply them.

Here are some other common incentive traps to avoid:

Rewarding individual performance over anything else. Imagine a sales team that hears, "Nothing is more important than hitting your personal quota." A member of that team is then presented with a choice to either undercut his colleague on a deal, which is easy to do, or try to land a new deal, which is harder. Based on these incentives, he will be better off if he chooses the former.

Rewarding short-term gains over long-term investments. Imagine an engineering team whose bonuses are determined every six months based on how many new features they've released. The manager has to decide between working on a number of lower-impact features or tackling the most-requested customer feature, which will take a year to build. The incentives suggest that she should pick the lower-impact features.

Rewarding lack of perceived issues or conflict. Imagine a manager who constantly talks about how happy he is that everyone on his team gets along. Whenever someone brings up a disagreement, he either dismisses it as "not a big deal" or expresses dissatisfaction that the issue exists in the first place. Over time, his team learns to hide their conflicts from him. Meanwhile, resentment and passive-aggressive behavior grows.

Rewarding the squeaky wheel. Imagine a manager whose report interviews at another company and gets a higher offer. The report says she'll leave unless she gets a raise to match. The manager says okay. The story gets out, and suddenly all the other members of the team feel incentivized to interview at other places.

The way to identify and resolve incentive traps is to regularly reflect on what the difference is between your stated values and how people are actually behaving on your team. What's leading them to make certain decisions? If you're not sure, ask. *Why did you choose to build these five features instead of the one that the customers are asking for?* If you learn the issue is primarily structural, make changes to your incentives so that the right behaviors are rewarded.

If the issue isn't structural, but someone does something that's out of line with your values, you must still take action. For example, maybe you care deeply about creating an atmosphere of respect within your team. One day, you hear someone shouting rudely at a teammate. If you do nothing, you risk sending the message that you tolerate this kind of behavior. Instead, defuse tensions in the moment by asking the shouter to calm down or help them leave the room. Later, in private, tell them that what they did is unacceptable.

When a report does something difficult that *is* in the spirit of your team's values—passing up a lucrative sales deal because of ethical concerns, firing a star performer who is creating a toxic work environment, or admitting openly when they've made a mistake—recognize them for it. Acknowledge that it was hard, and thank them for doing the right thing.

INVENT TRADITIONS THAT CELEBRATE YOUR VALUES

Not long after I started at Facebook, I decided to join a group of engineers for lunch. As I approached, I saw that they were in the middle of a vigorous debate. One of them had proposed an idea for a new feature he was sure would change the world. Others weren't so convinced. "I can't imagine myself using that in a million years," someone retorted. He motioned to me as I sat down. "What do you think, Julie?" Half a dozen heads turned in my direction. "Hmm . . ." I took a sip of soup, trying to figure out how to gracefully extricate

myself from being a deciding vote on a topic I had next to no context on.

Happily, someone else jumped in. "Well, why don't you build
this feature and we'll see?" "Yeah!" another voice agreed. "Do it at
the next hackathon!"

I learned then that a *hackathon* was a storied company tradition. The goal was to come in and spend a few dedicated hours creating a prototype of an idea you were excited about. Whether
alone or with a handful of others, you were encouraged to build
whatever you thought was good for the company. Hackathons
were known for their buzzy energy, often lasting into the wee
hours of the night until you could wave your colleagues over to see
a live, working version of the thing in your head.

Hackathons resulted in some well-known and successful
products—chat and video, among others. But more than that,
they were a fun way to bring people together and make concrete
Facebook's earliest values: "Be Bold" and "Move Fast."

There is power in rituals. Beyond slogans or speeches, they create actions around which team members can bond. And they can
be as unique, quirky, and fun as your team.

I love learning about the different traditions teams have to celebrate their values. Here are some examples:

- Personal prompts (like "Favorite childhood movie" or "Best
  gift you ever received at Christmas") at the start of a meeting
  so people can get to know their teammates better
- Monthly "Learn how to paint/sculpt/craft" nights to encourage creativity and beginner's mindset
- A gigantic "customer love" stuffed teddy bear awarded to the
  person who went above and beyond to help a customer in the
  past month
- An annual Oscars-style award ceremony so people can recognize all the ways in which their coworkers are awesome

- Monday morning yoga sessions to promote mindfulness
- "Fail of the week," where people share their mistakes in a safe forum to encourage authenticity and learning

One of the things Mark Zuckerberg has continued to do for more than ten years is hold an internal Q&A on Friday afternoons, where anybody at the company can ask him any question and get an honest answer. These questions can be about Facebook's future direction, recent decisions Mark made, company policies, or even Mark's personal opinions on the latest news. Some of these questions can be extremely direct—for example, "X seems like a bad idea—why are we doing it?"

At an organization as big as Facebook, there are thousands of demands on the CEO's time. And yet Mark continues to stand in front of the company every week talking about whatever people choose to bring up. Why? Because one of Facebook's greatest values is openness. If he doesn't set an example, why should anyone else believe it's important?

As a leader, nurturing culture may not be the first thing on your mind. You may be dreaming about the changes you want to create in the world or sketching out the master strategy that will get you there. But success or failure aren't usually the results of a few sweeping decisions. Rather, how far you get will be the sum of the millions of actions taken by your team during the small, quotidian moments. How does everyone treat each other? How do you solve problems together? What are you willing to give up to act in accordance with your values?

Pay attention to your own actions—the little things you say and do—as well as what behaviors you are rewarding or discouraging. All of it works together to tell the story of what you care about and how you believe a great team should work together.

The Journey Is 1% Finished

THE MYTH

THE REALITY

When I look back on my management path thus far, it looks like a toddler's attempt at drawing a straight line—full of squiggles, swerves, and mistaken meanderings. There are countless instances where I look back and wince, remembering how I handled things, remembering that ever-present taste in my mouth of inexperience and expectation, confusion and ambition.

There were late nights spent over chat arguing about some incredibly trivial issue, my blood pressure spiking as the words blinked onto the screen, shorter and sharper with each volley. There were 1:1s where neither of us would hear the other, a *Game of Thrones*–esque wall between us. There were meetings where I slouched in the back, surly because I thought I was right and everybody else was wrong. I've had people break down in tears in front of me while I stammered like a malfunctioning robot. I've had months when I couldn't meet my own manager's eyes without bursting into tears myself.

There were so many instances where I didn't feel experienced enough, farsighted enough, empathetic enough, determined enough, or patient enough. As a result, projects faltered. Misunderstandings festered. And people I cared about left feeling like I let them down.

But I was lucky. I learned how to manage in one of the most dynamic environments in the world, under some of the best leadership of our era. My managers believed in me. My colleagues showed me how to strive for better. And my team inspired me.

If you take a walk around the Facebook office, you'll see that there are no bare white walls. The ceilings are open and unfinished, exposing pipes and bundles of wires. Our space is covered with art and the artifacts of our culture. There are flyers about upcoming hackathons, images of our newest data centers, and reminders to "Be Bold" and that "Nothing at Facebook Is Somebody Else's Problem." My favorite is a poster with big orange capital letters. I have a smaller version sitting on my desk at home too. It reads: *The Journey Is 1% Finished*.

In another ten years, I know I'll look back and realize that the path I'm on today is still squiggly. There is much left to learn, and I am far from being the manager I aspire to be. But with time, will, and a growth mindset, the lessons ahead are right there for my taking.

Recently, I was having a 1:1 with a new manager. We were talking about her observations a few weeks in—the challenges of stepping into a new environment, the differences between this place and her last job, the opportunities to do meaningful work. Then she gave me one of the best compliments I've ever received: "You've built a great team, and I'm excited to be a part of it."

A group of people working in unison is a wonderful thing to behold. Done well, it ceases to be about you or me, one individual or another. Instead, you feel the energy of dozens or hundreds or even thousands of hearts and minds directed toward a shared purpose, guided by shared values. If you or I do our jobs well, then our teams will thrive. We will build something that will outlast us, that will be made stronger by all who become a part of it.

Good luck in your path ahead. Go out with your team and make something wonderful together.

Acknowledgments

Any big journey is a team effort, and this book is no exception. If not for Stephanie Frerich and Leah Trouwborst and the seeds that they cast from that very first phone call, this whole thing never would have happened. Thank you for your exuberance from day one, and for making it click for me what I should write about and why I should do it now (and not in twenty years). Your voices helped my own voice shine, and your unwavering support gave me the wind at my back.

I'm grateful to Lisa DiMona for helping me navigate the fine waters of being a first-time author. Years before we met, Writers House was my dream agency, and you've been the best champion anyone could ask for.

Dan McGinn—your editing prowess, deep research expertise, and writing advice were so valuable to me, and I found myself becoming a better manager through working with you and learning from your insights. Thanks for always checking in, even at the eleventh hour.

Pablo Stanley—I've loved your quirky comics for ages and I'm so glad we got to work together on this project. Thanks to you, a giraffe will now pop into my head whenever I think of typical "managers." And Kimberly Glyder, I have so much gratitude for this amazing cover done under amazing grace (and tight constraints!).

To my dearest friends and earliest readers: Lauren Luk, thank you for prodding me to get over my tech jargon, and for our Indian dance breaks. Anjali Khurana, thank you for your generous notes (served hand in hand with your generous baked goods). Every pop culture reference was written with you in mind. Marie Lu, I'm pretty sure I wouldn't be a writer *or* a designer if not for our friendship and our childhood adventures. Grateful for your advice on titles, the biz, and letting go of sentences that still sound weird to me.

Feedback is a gift, and I'm incredibly thankful for everyone who has generously provided it on earlier drafts of this book: Charlie Sutton, your sage stylistic notes and pinboarding enthusiasm will not be long forgotten; Matt Kelly, I loved your meta-meeting notes and the gentle reminders of what I shouldn't forget; Jason Leimgruber, your level of thoughtfulness and detail blew me away, and I jumped at the challenge of living up to your feedback; Anita Patwardhan Butler, you helped me clarify some hugely important concepts; Moneta Ho Kushner, the book became sharper and more precise because of you; Mary-Lynne Williams, we both hate those squiggly lines, so thanks for suggesting better ways to frame things; Tutti Taygerly, I'm glad you helped me realize *expectational* shouldn't be a real word; Chelsea Klukas, thanks for your probing questions; Kaisha Hom, your messages made my night as I edited with bleary eyes. Will Ruben and Callie Schweitzer, your last-minute suggestions were so on point.

To my fellow Facebookers, past and present: a company is the sum of its people, and the greatest privilege of my past twelve years is working alongside you. I'm especially grateful for the folks who gave me the opportunity to do what I do: Wayne Chang—your stories of that tight-knit group on University Ave. who shipped often, dreamed big, and knew how to have fun proved irresistible. Thanks for being an amazing recruiter and an even better friend. Rebekah Cox, thanks for taking a leap of faith on an unproven young designer and for keeping the ground steady enough for me to learn to stand. Kate Aronowitz, you've taught me so much, but most important that both design and management always go back to people. Chris Cox, thank you for imbuing a deep humanity in everything you do, and for helping me realize time and time again that the bar can always be raised. Will Cathcart, you have such a gift for bringing people together, clarifying what matters, and doing it all with wit and humility.

I also want to give a special thanks to my friends and colleagues whom I've worked the closest with over the years and from whom I have learned so much: Tom Alison, Kang-Xin Jin, Fidji Simo, Adam Mosseri, Chandra Narayanan, Ronan Bradley, Annette Reavis, Deborah Liu, Jennifer Dulski, John Hegeman, Rushabh Doshi, and David Ginsberg—I'm constantly in awe of your superpowers and proud to be a part of your crew. Stacy McCarthy, thank you for helping me find my center. Robyn Morris, Drew Hamlin, Margaret Stewart, Luke Woods, Jessica Watson, Austin Bales, John Evans, Joey Flynn, Francis Luu, Geoff Teehan, Amanda Linden, Jon Lax, David Gillis, Alex Cornell, Caitlin Winner, Nathan Borror, Laura Javier, Nan Gao, Aaron Sittig, Brandon Walkin, Mike Matas, Sharon Matas, Christopher Clare, and Dantley Davis—I'm a better designer and manager because of you. Andrew Bosworth, Alex Schultz, Mark Rabkin, Naomi Gleit, Caryn Marooney, Javier Olivan, Ami Vora, Kevin Systrom, Mike Krieger, and Mike Schroepfer—thank you for the conversations, notes, and lessons that have illuminated for me what strong leadership looks like. Sheryl Sandberg, thank you for showing me how to lead with strength, deep caring, and uncompromising authenticity. And Mark Zuckerberg, thank you for teaching me to dream bigger, question every assumption, and look way, *way* further ahead.

To my team, past and present: You are my greatest teachers. You paint the vision and you sew the seams of quality. Every day, I'm inspired by the thousands upon thousands of details that you sweat in the name of creating a wonderful user experience that brings people closer together.

And finally, to my family: Mike, thank you for being my favorite human and for exploring dozens of new playgrounds (and Irish festivals!) with our kids on weekends when I needed some alone time with this manuscript; Dad, thank you for passing down to me your love of books and for being proud of me for everything I've ever written, even those terrible third-grade essays; Mom, I love people because you love people. Thank you for sneaking your most important empathy lessons into those family stories you'd tell me every Saturday after lunch. And finally, a huge thank-you to my kids, who put up with their fair share of "Mommy-computer time." I love you to the moon and back, and I hope you'll find this book useful someday.

Notes

CHAPTER ONE: WHAT IS MANAGEMENT?

20 **"the *output* of the work unit":** Andrew S. Grove, *High Output Management* (New York: Vintage Books, 2015), 17.

21 **"Research consistently shows that teams underperform":** Diane Coutu, "Why Teams Don't Work," *Harvard Business Review*, May 2009, https://hbr.org/2009/05/why-teams-dont-work.

21 **Hackman's research describes five conditions:** J. Richard Hackman, *Leading Teams: Setting the Stage for Great Performances* (Boston: Harvard Business School, 2002), ix.

27 **known today as Maslow's hierarchy of needs:** A. H. Maslow, "A Theory of Human Motivation," *Psychological Review* 50, no. 4 (1943): 370–96.

30 **plenty of other managers:** John Rampton, "23 of the Most Amazingly Successful Introverts in History," *Inc.*, July 20, 2015, https://www.inc.com/john-rampton/23-amazingly-successful-introverts-throughout-history.html.

34 **"What makes a good leader:** Simon Sinek, *Leaders Eat Last* (New York: Portfolio, 2017), 83.

CHAPTER THREE: LEADING A SMALL TEAM

58 **He flips the question around and asks:** Grove, *High Output Management*, 157.

60 **"You must trust people":** Anton Chekhov, *The Greatest Works of Anton Chekhov* (Prague: e-artnow ebooks, 2015).

61 **feel a little awkward:** See also Mark Rabkin, "The Art of the Awkward 1:1," *Medium*, November 1, 2016, accessed March 9, 2018, https://medium.com/@mrabkin/the-art-of-the-awkward-1-1-f4e1 dcbd1c5c.

69 **"Vulnerability sounds like truth":** Brené Brown, *Daring Greatly: How the Courage to Be Vulnerable Transforms the Way We Live, Love, Parent, and Lead* (New York: Penguin Random House, 2015), 37.

72 **"There is one quality":** Marcus Buckingham, "What Great Managers Do," *Harvard Business Review*, March 2005, https://hbr.org/2005 /03/what-great-managers-do.

73 **He defines an asshole:** Robert I. Sutton, *The No Asshole Rule: Building a Civilized Workplace and Surviving One That Isn't* (New York: Business Plus, 2010), 9.

78 **"What I think is brutal and 'false kindness'":** Jack Welch, *Jack: Straight from the Gut* (New York: Warner Books, 2001), 161–62.

79 **"Are we shooting people?":** Vivian Giang, "Why We Need to Stop Thinking of Getting Fired as a Bad Thing," *Fast Company*, March 16, 2016, https://www.fastcompany.com/3057796/why-we-need-to-stop -thinking-of-getting-fired-as-a-bad-thing.

CHAPTER FOUR: THE ART OF FEEDBACK

96 **"heart rate and blood pressure":** Harvard Business Review, *HBR Guide to Delivering Effective Feedback* (Boston: Harvard Business Review Press, 2016), 11.

103 **"It's brutally hard to tell people":** Kim Scott, *Radical Candor: Be a Kick-Ass Boss without Losing Your Humanity* (New York: St. Martin's Press, 2017), xi.

CHAPTER FIVE: MANAGING YOURSELF

110 **"Ask any new manager about the early days":** Linda A. Hill, "Becoming the Boss," *Harvard Business Review*, January 2007, https:// hbr.org/2007/01/becoming-the-boss.

114 *the Dunning-Kruger effect*: Justin Kruger and David Dunning, "Unskilled and Unaware of It: How Difficulties in Recognizing

One's Own Incompetence Lead to Inflated Self-Assessments," *Journal of Personality and Social Psychology*, American Psychological Association 77 (6): 1121–34.

117   **In her influential book *Mindset*:** Carol Dweck, *Mindset: The New Psychology of Success* (New York: Random House, 2006).

125   **group of basketball players:** Alan Richardson, "Mental Practice: A Review and Discussion Part I," *Research Quarterly*, American Association for Health, Physical Education and Recreation 38, no. 1 (1967).

125   **imagined themselves working out:** Guang H. Yue and Kelly J. Cole, "Strength Increases from the Motor Program: Comparison of Training with Maximal Voluntary and Imagined Muscle," *Journal of Neurophysiology* 67, no. 5 (1992): 1114–23.

125   **"I never hit a shot":** Jack Nicklaus with Ken Bowden, *Golf My Way: The Instructional Classic, Revised and Updated* (London: Simon & Schuster, 2005), 79.

126   **Reese Witherspoon confessing:** Reese Witherspoon, "Reese Witherspoon Shares Her Lean In Story," Lean In, accessed March 12, 2018, https://leanin.org/stories/reese-witherspoon.

128   **reported coping better:** Linda Farris Kurtz, "Mutual Aid for Affective Disorders: The Manic Depressive and Depressive Association," *American Journal of Orthopsychiatry* 58, no. 1 (1988): 152–55.

129   **write down five things:** Robert A. Emmons, *Thanks! How Practicing Gratitude Can Make You Happier* (Boston: Houghton Mifflin, 2008), 27–35.

129   **high workplace stress:** Reg Talbot, Cary Cooper, and Steve Barrow, "Creativity and Stress," *Creativity and Innovation Management* 1, no. 4 (1992): 183–93.

129   **"when people were feeling":** Karen Weintraub, "How Creativity Can Help Reduce Stress," *Boston Globe*, April 24, 2014, https://www.bostonglobe.com/lifestyle/health-wellness/2015/04/24/how-creativity-can-help-reduce-stress/iEJta3lapaaFxZY6wfv5UK/story.html.

135   **couple our experiences with periodic reflections:** Giada Di Stefano, Francesca Gino, Gary P. Pisano, and Bradley R. Staats, "Making Experience Count: The Role of Reflection in Individual Learning," Harvard Business School NOM Unit Working Paper No. 14-093; Harvard Business School Technology & Operations Mgt. Unit Working Paper No. 14-093; HEC Paris Research Paper No. SPE-2016-1181, June 14, 2016.

CHAPTER SIX: AMAZING MEETINGS

142 **chief executives spend:** Oriana Bandiera, Luigi Guiso, Andrea
Prat, and Raffaella Sadun, "What Do CEOs Do?," No. 11-081, Harvard Business School Working Paper, February 25, 2011, https://
hbswk.hbs.edu/item/what-do-ceos-do.

142 **a single executive meeting:** Michael Mankins, "This Weekly Meeting Took Up 300,000 Hours a Year," *Harvard Business Review*, April
29, 2014, https://hbr.org/2014/04/how-a-weekly-meeting-took-up
-300000-hours-a-year.

142 **"Happy families are all alike":** Leo Tolstoy, *Anna Karenina* (New
York: Random House, 2000).

145 **"disagree and commit":** Jeff Bezos, "2016 Letter to Shareholders,"
About Amazon (blog), Amazon.com, April 17, 2017, https://www.am
azon.com/p/feature/z6o9g6sysxur57t.

147 **whatever comes to mind isn't actually effective:** Tomas Chamorro-
Premuzic, "Why Group Brainstorming Is a Waste of Time," *Harvard
Business Review*, March 25, 2015, https://hbr.org/2015/03/why
-group-brainstorming-is-a-waste-of-time.

158 **71 percent found their meetings:** Leslie A. Perlow, Constance
Noonan Hadley, and Eunice Eun, "Stop the Meeting Madness,"
Harvard Business Review, July/August 2017, https://hbr.org/2017
/07/stop-the-meeting-madness.

158 **"trigger employee exhaustion":** Nale Lehmann-Willenbrock, Ste-
ven G. Rogelberg, Joseph A. Allen, and John E. Kello, "The Critical
Importance of Meetings to Leader and Organizational Success:
Evidence-Based Insights and Implications for Key Stakeholders,"
Organizational Dynamics 47, no. 1 (2017): 32–36.

CHAPTER SEVEN: HIRING WELL

168 **"people can easily toggle":** Patty McCord, "How to Hire," *Harvard
Business Review*, January/February 2018, https://hbr.org/2018/01
/how-to-hire.

170 **"a complete random mess":** Adam Bryant, "In Head-Hunting, Big
Data May Not Be Such a Big Deal," *New York Times*, June 19, 2013.

171 **American symphonies implemented:** Claudia Goldin and Cecilia
Rouse, "Orchestrating Impartiality: The Impact of 'Blind' Auditions on Female Musicians," *American Economic Review* 90, no. 4
(2000): 715–41.

171 **"your ability to perform at Google"**: Bryant, "Head-Hunting."

172 **"undervalue the reference check"**: Kevin Ryan, "Gilt Groupe's CEO on Building a Team of A Players," *Harvard Business Review*, January 2012, https://hbr.org/2012/01/gilt-groupes-ceo-on-building-a-team-of-a-players.

177 **financial returns higher than average:** Vivian Hunt, Dennis Layton, and Sara Prince, "Diversity Matters," McKinsey & Company, February 2, 2015, https://assets.mckinsey.com/~/media/857F440109AA 4D13A54D9C496D86ED58.ashx.

177 **one female board member:** Credit Suisse Research Institute, *Gender Diversity and Corporate Performance*, 2012.

178 **teams consisting of an "outsider":** Katherine W. Phillips, Katie A. Liljenquist, and Margaret A. Neale, "Is the Pain Worth the Gain? The Advantages and Liabilities of Agreeing with Socially Distinct Newcomers," *Personality and Social Psychology Bulletin* 35, no. 3 (2009): 336–50.

186 **"giving away your LEGOs"**: "'Give Away Your Legos' and Other Commandments for Scaling Startups," *First Round Review*, http://firstround.com/review/give-away-your-legos-and-other-commandments-for-scaling-startups.

CHAPTER EIGHT: MAKING THINGS HAPPEN

193 **Hoover never said this:** Paul Dickson, *Words from the White House: Words and Phrases Coined or Popularized by America's Presidents* (New York: Walker & Company, 2013), 43.

195 **"Plans are worthless"**: William M. Blair, "President Draws Planning Moral: Recalls Army Days to Show Value of Preparedness in Time of Crisis," *New York Times,* November 15, 1957, https://www.nytimes.com/1957/11/15/archives/president-draws-planning-moral-recalls-army-days-to-show-value-of.html.

197 **"Few people take objectives"**: Richard Koch, *The 80/20 Principle: The Secret to Achieving More with Less* (New York: Currency, 1998), 145.

198 **"People think focus means:** "America's Most Admired Companies: Steve Jobs Speaks Out," *Fortune*, March 7, 2008, http://archive.fortune.com/galleries/2008/fortune/0803/gallery.jobsqna.fortune/6.html.

200 **"Work expands so as:** Cyril Northcote Parkinson, "Parkinson's Law," *Economist*, November 19, 1955, https://www.economist.com/news/1955/11/19/parkinsons-law.

201 **the planning fallacy:** Daniel Kahneman and Amos Tversky, "Intuitive Prediction: Biases and Corrective Procedures," *TIMS Studies in Management Science* 12 (1979): 313–27.

202 **"Work contracts to fit:** Mark Horstman and Michael Auzenne, "Horstman's Law of Project Management," Manager Tools, accessed March 18, 2018, https://www.manager-tools.com/2009/01 /horstman's-law-project-management-part-1-hall-fame-guidance.

204 **"Most decisions should probably be made":** Bezos, "2016 Letter to Shareholders."

206 **"If you don't know where you are going":** Matt Bonesteel, "The Best Things Yogi Berra Ever Said," *Washington Post*, September 24, 2015, https://www.washingtonpost.com/news/early-lead/wp/2015 /09/23/the-best-things-yogi-berra-ever-said.

208 **"Be earth's most customer-centric":** Patrick Hull, "Be Visionary. Think Big.," *Forbes*, December 19, 2012, accessed March 18, 2018, https://www.forbes.com/sites/patrickhull/2012/12/19/be-visionary -think-big/#ee5d8723c175.

208 **"respected car company in America":** "What Are Toyota's Mission and Vision Statements?," FAQs: Frequently Asked Questions for All Things Toyota, Toyota, accessed March 18, 2018, http://toyota .custhelp.com/app/answers/detail/a_id/7654/~/what-are-toyotas -mission-and-vision-statements%3F.

209 **"Nearly everyone else wanted to sell":** Mark Zuckerberg, "Mark Zuckerberg's Commencement Address at Harvard," Address, Harvard 366th Commencement Address, Cambridge, MA, May 25, 2017, https://news.harvard.edu/gazette/story/2017/05/mark-zuckerbergs -speech-as-written-for-harvards-class-of-2017.

213 **"No man ever steps":** Heraclitus, *Fragments*, trans. Brooks Haxton (New York: Penguin Classics, 2003).

CHAPTER NINE: LEADING A GROWING TEAM

227 **"We control the world":** Yuval Noah Harari, interview by Arun Rath, *All Things Considered*, February 7, 2015, https://www.npr .org/2015/02/07/383276672/from-hunter-gatherers-to-space -explorers-a-70-000-year-story.

230 **"The subordinate did poor work":** Grove, *High Output Management*, 177.

Index